GEHRY×FUTAGAWA

Photographed by Yukio Futagawa
Edited by Yoshio Futagawa
Designed by Takuya Seki

Copyright © 2015 A.D.A. EDITA Tokyo Co., Ltd.
3-12-14 Sendagaya, Shibuya-ku, Tokyo 151-0051, Japan
All rights reserved. No part of this publication may be reproduced,
stored in a retrieval system, or transmitted,
in any form or by any means, electronic, mechanical,
photocopying, recording, or otherwise,
without permission in writing from the publisher.

Copyright of photographs © 2015 GA photographers

Printed and bound in Japan

ISBN 978-4-87140-494-5 C1052

GEHRY×FUTAGAWA

Best of Frank O. Gehry by Yukio Futagawa

VITRA INTERNATIONAL FURNITURE DESIGN MUSEUM 1987-89

CHIAT/DAY MAIN STREET 1985-91

WALT DISNEY CONCERT HALL 1989-2003

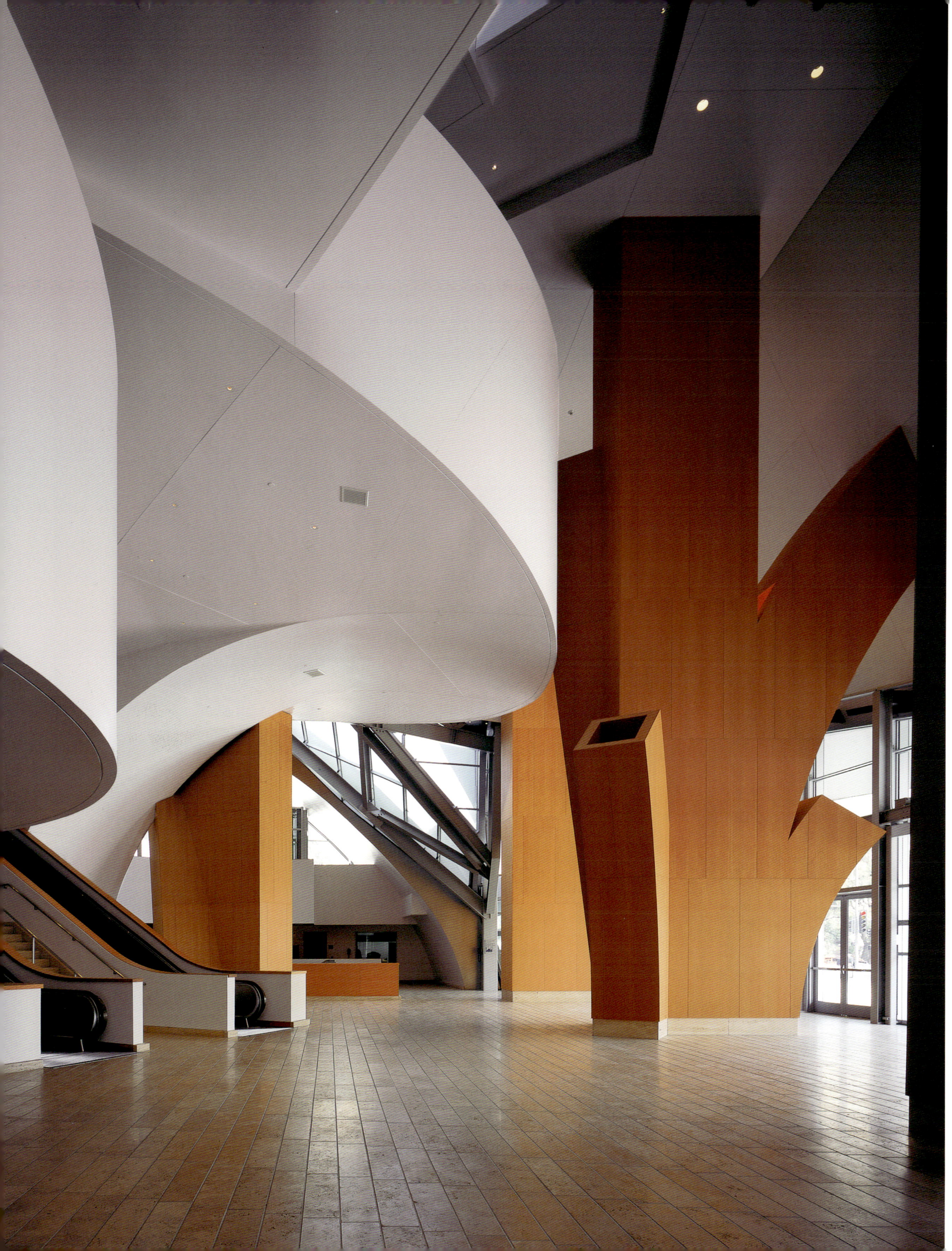

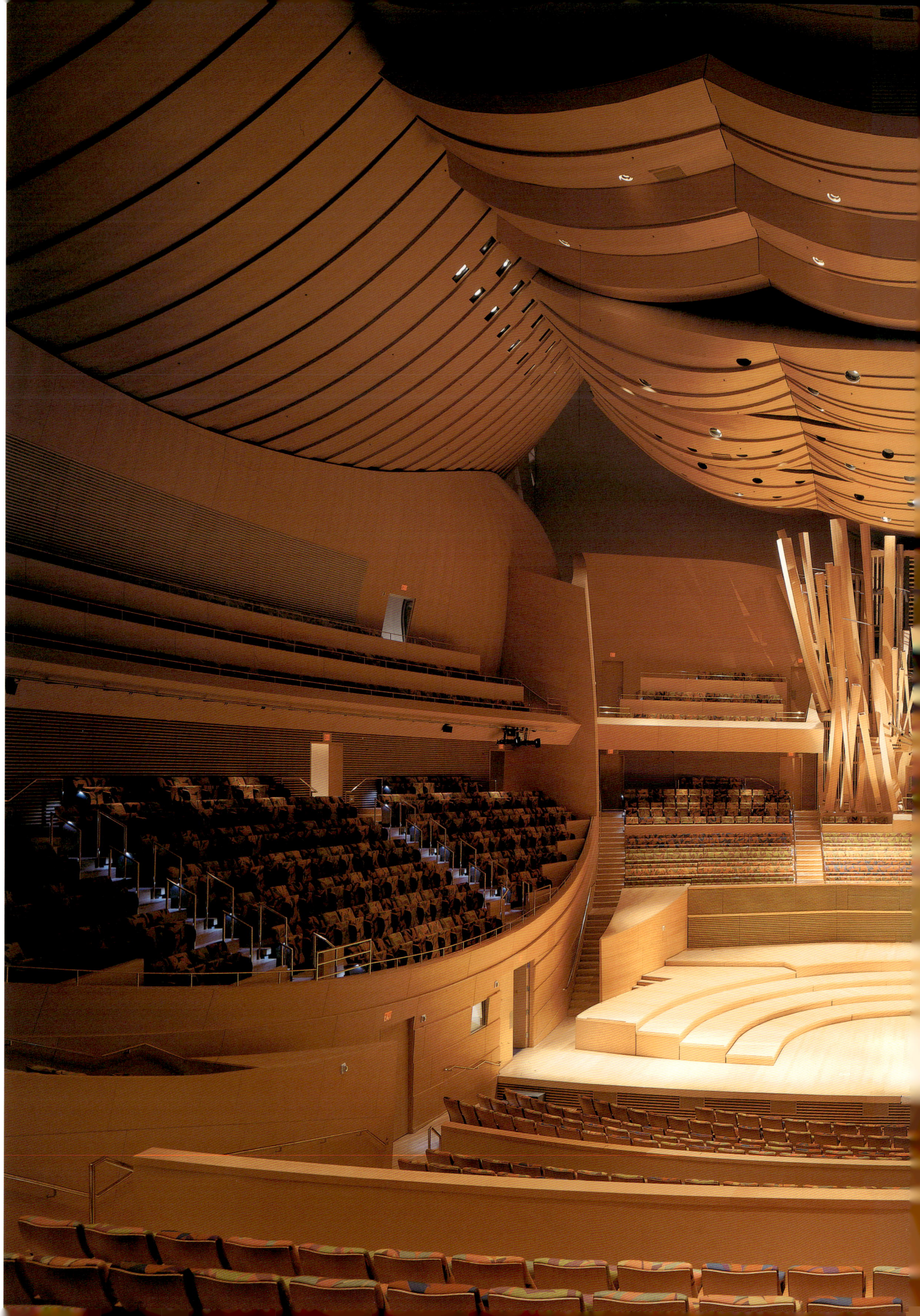

37

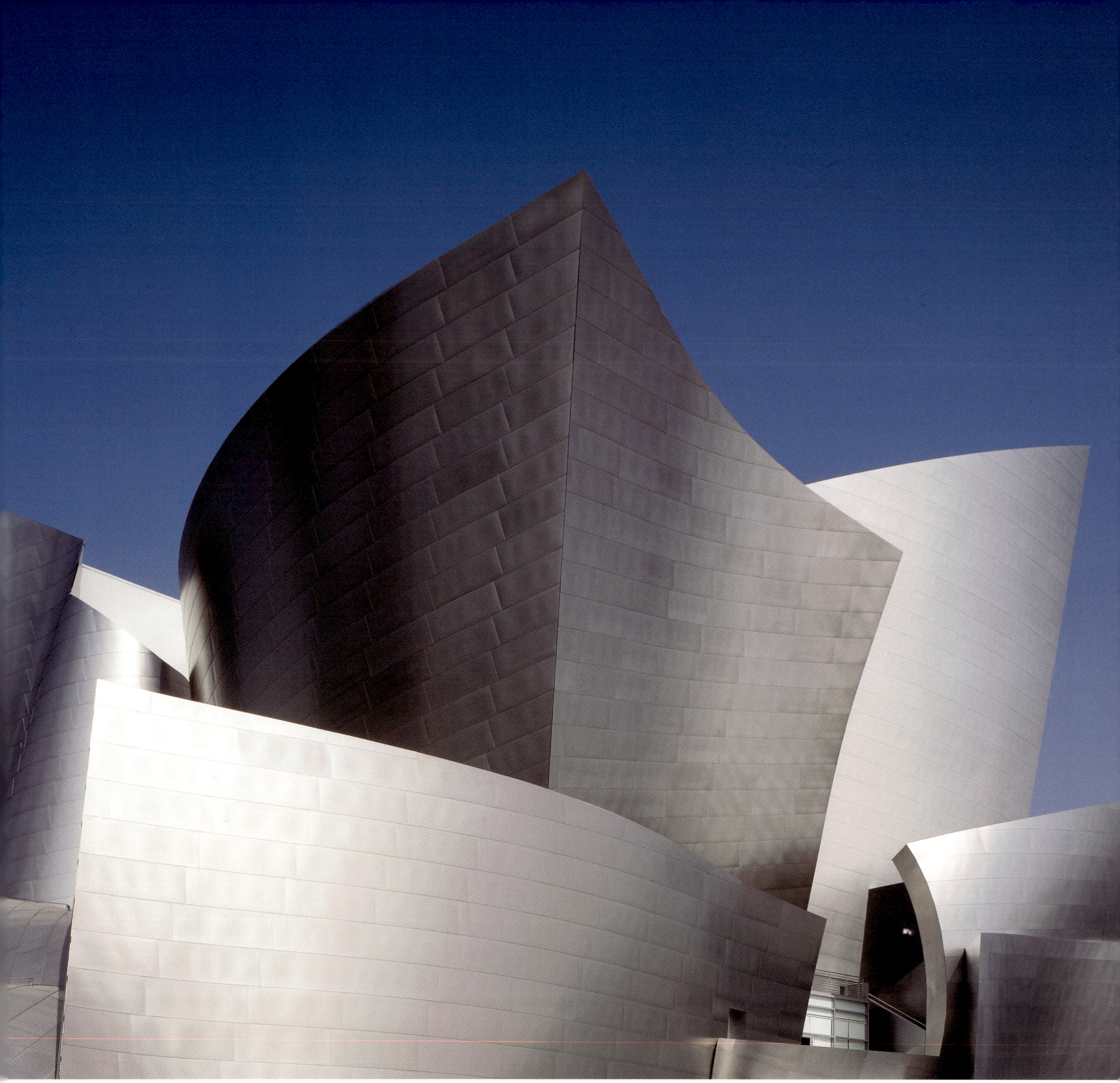

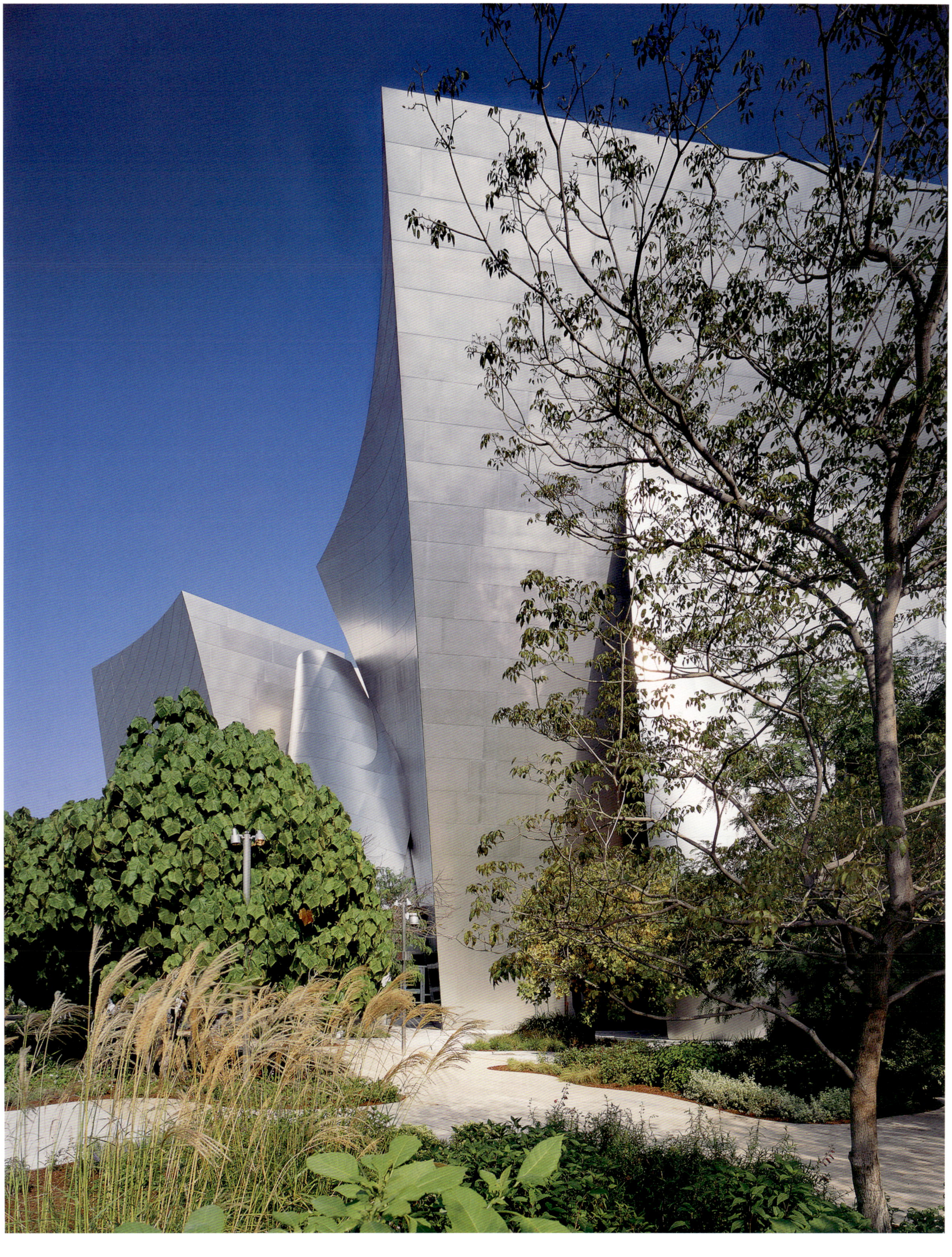

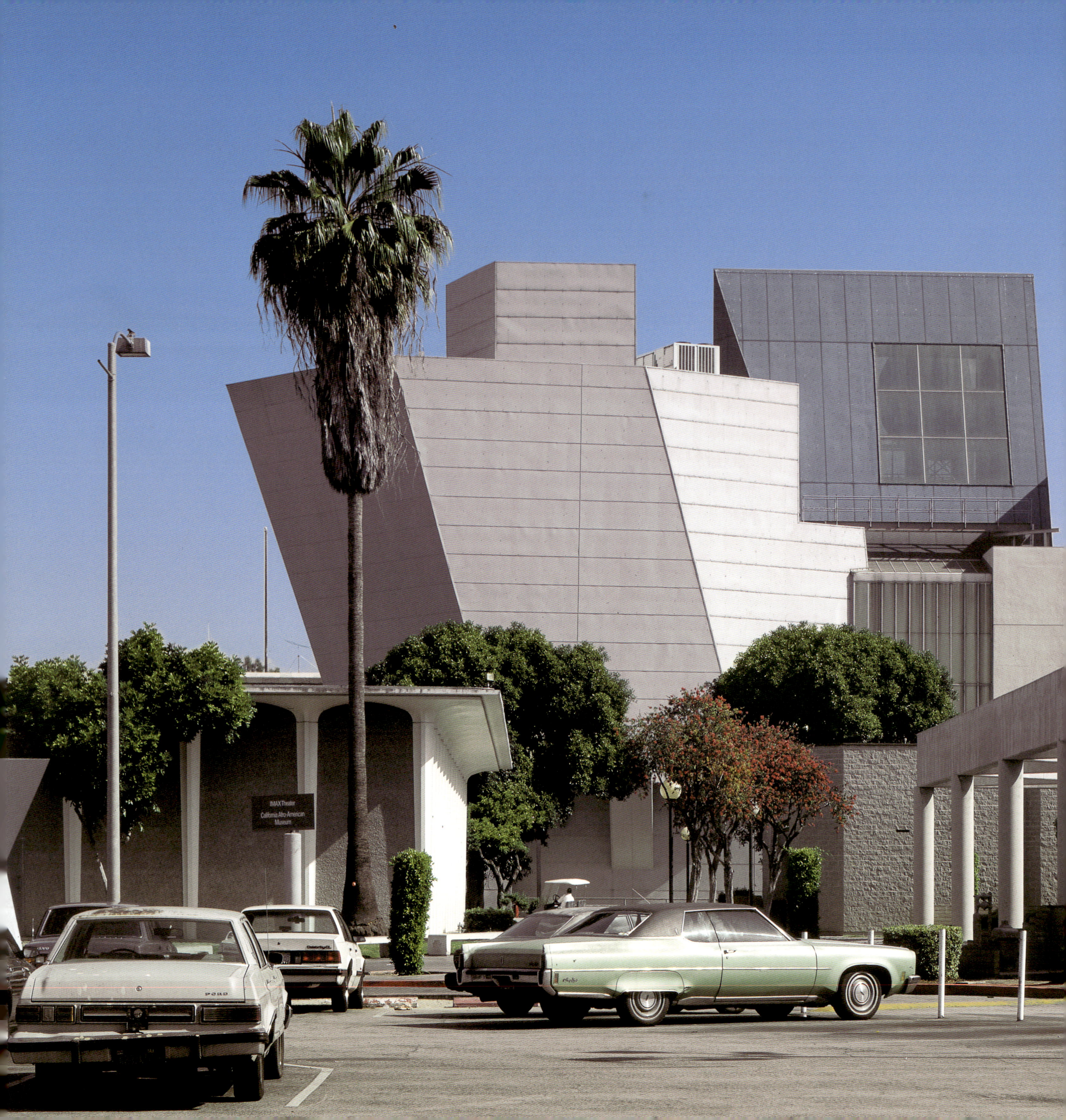
IMAX Theater
California Afro-American
Museum

CALIFORNIA AEROSPACE MUSEUM AND THEATER   1982-84

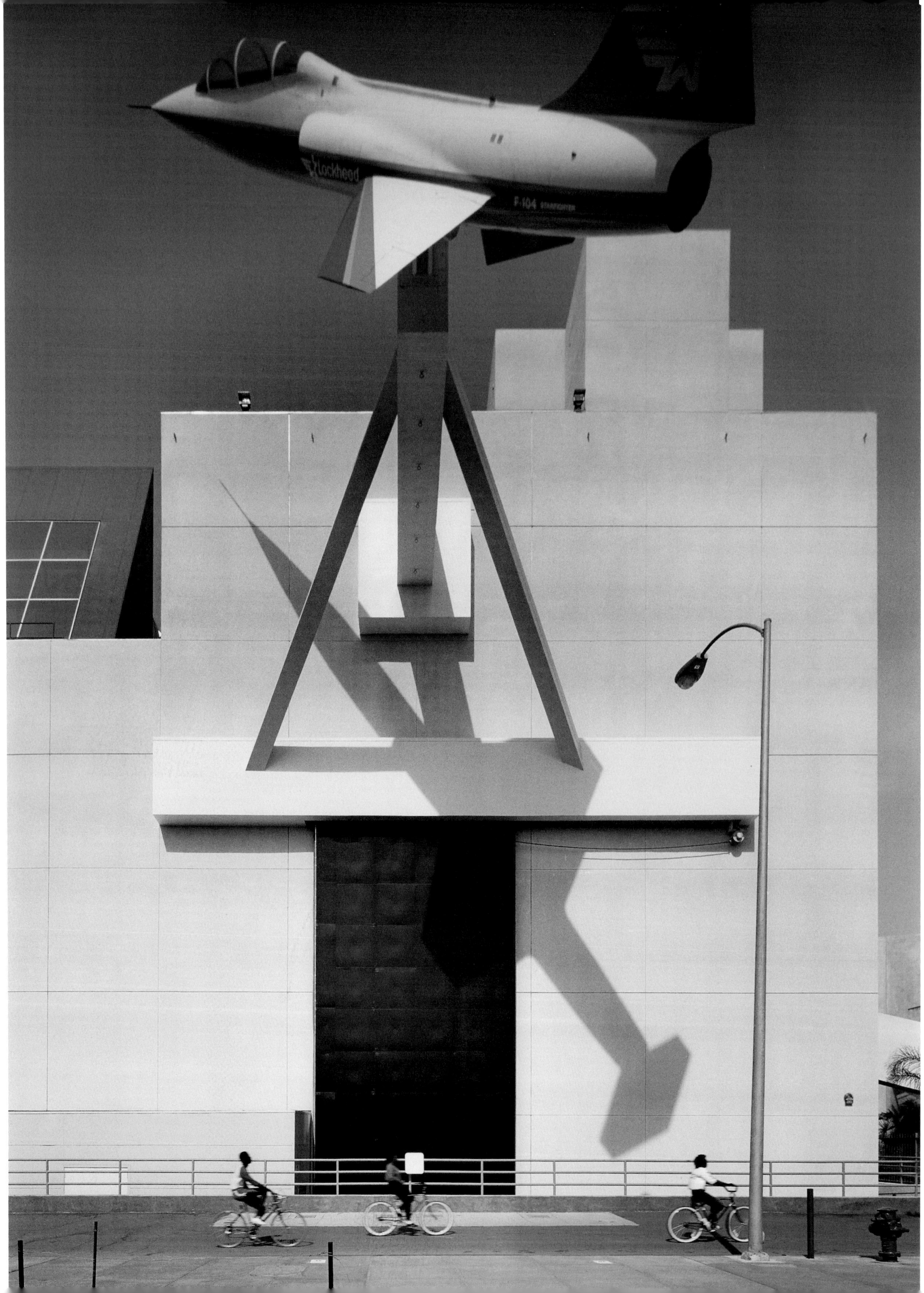
Lockheed
F-104

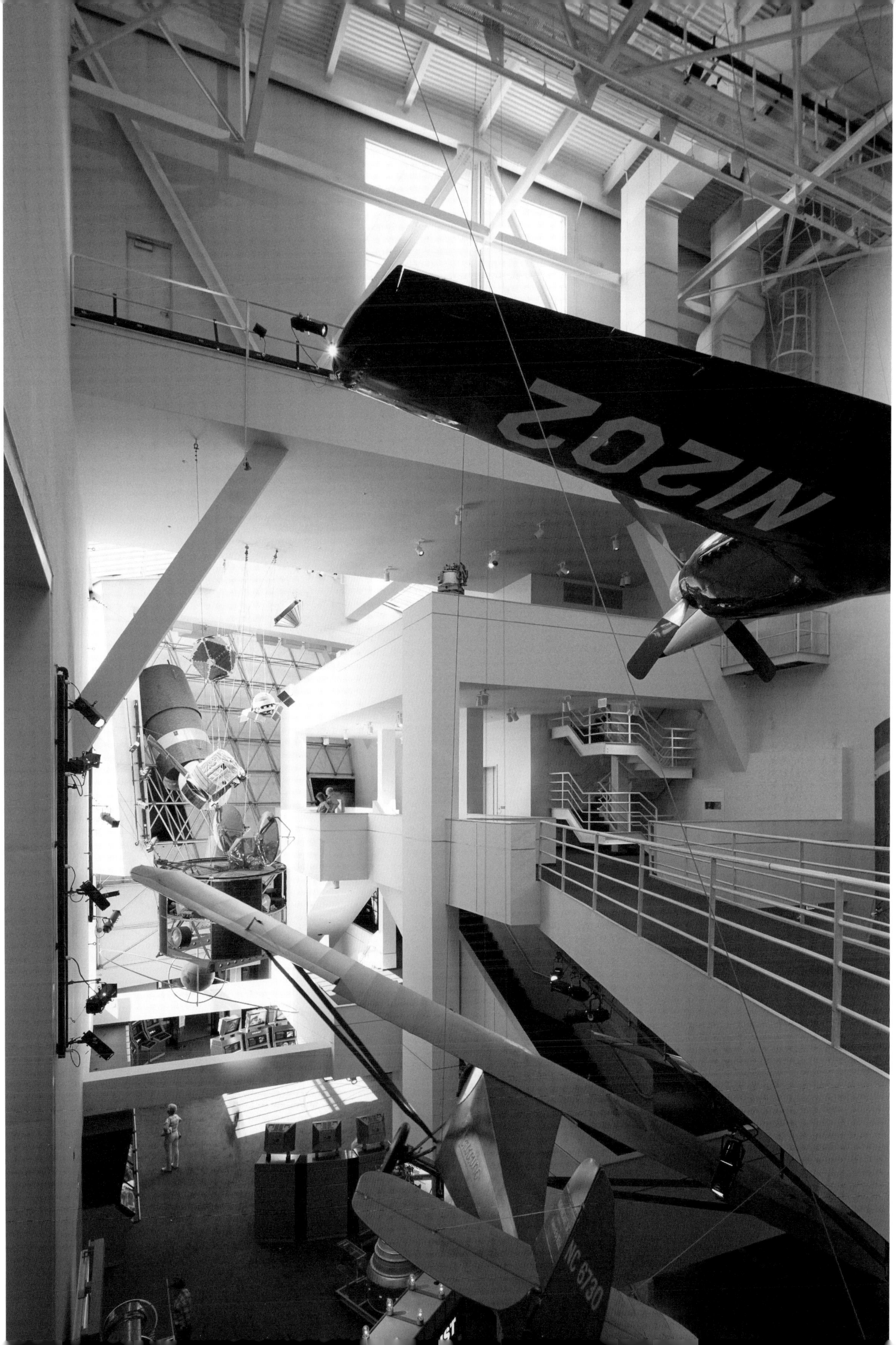
N1202

44

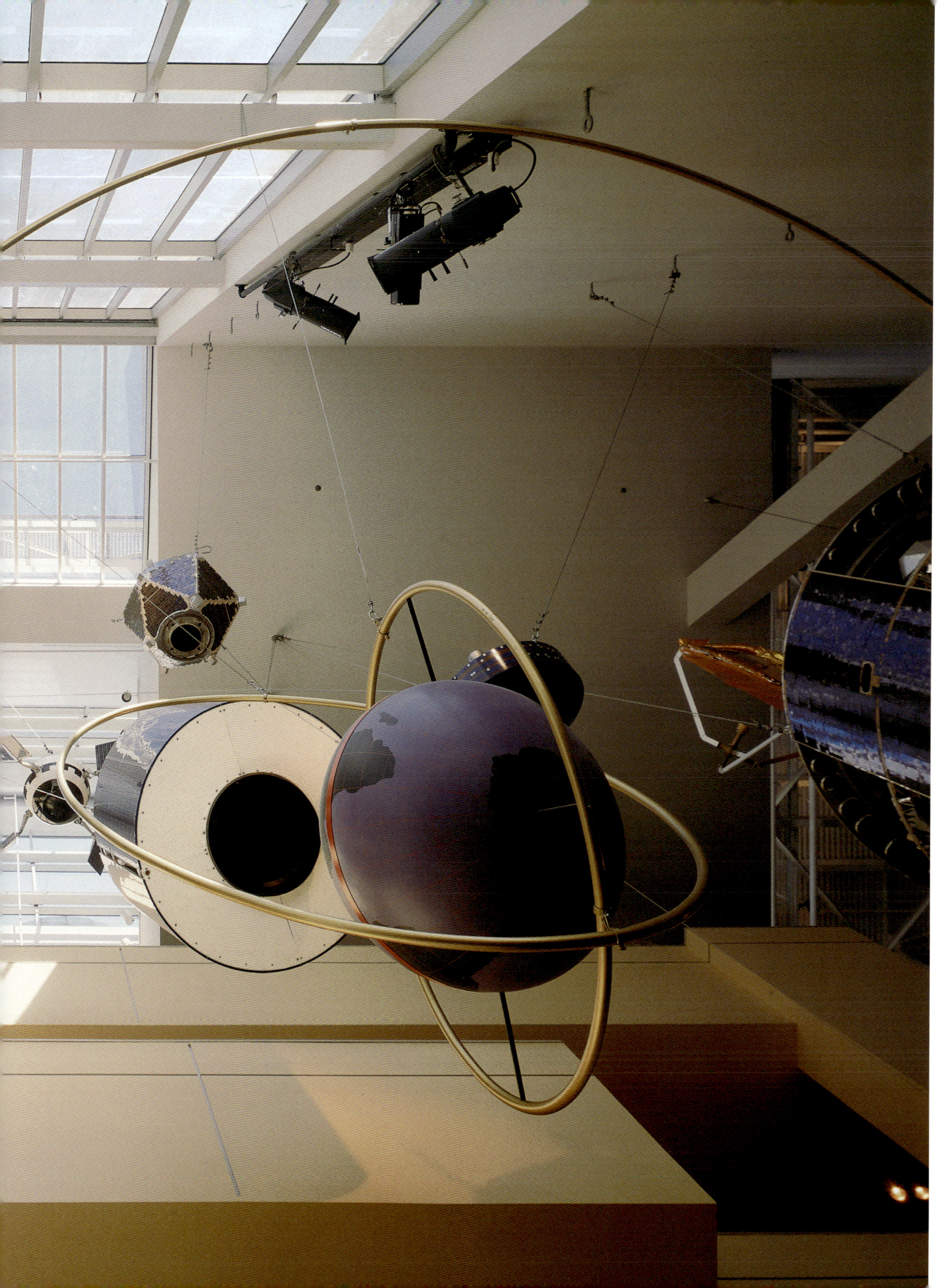

GEHRY RESIDENCE 1977-78, 1991-94

47

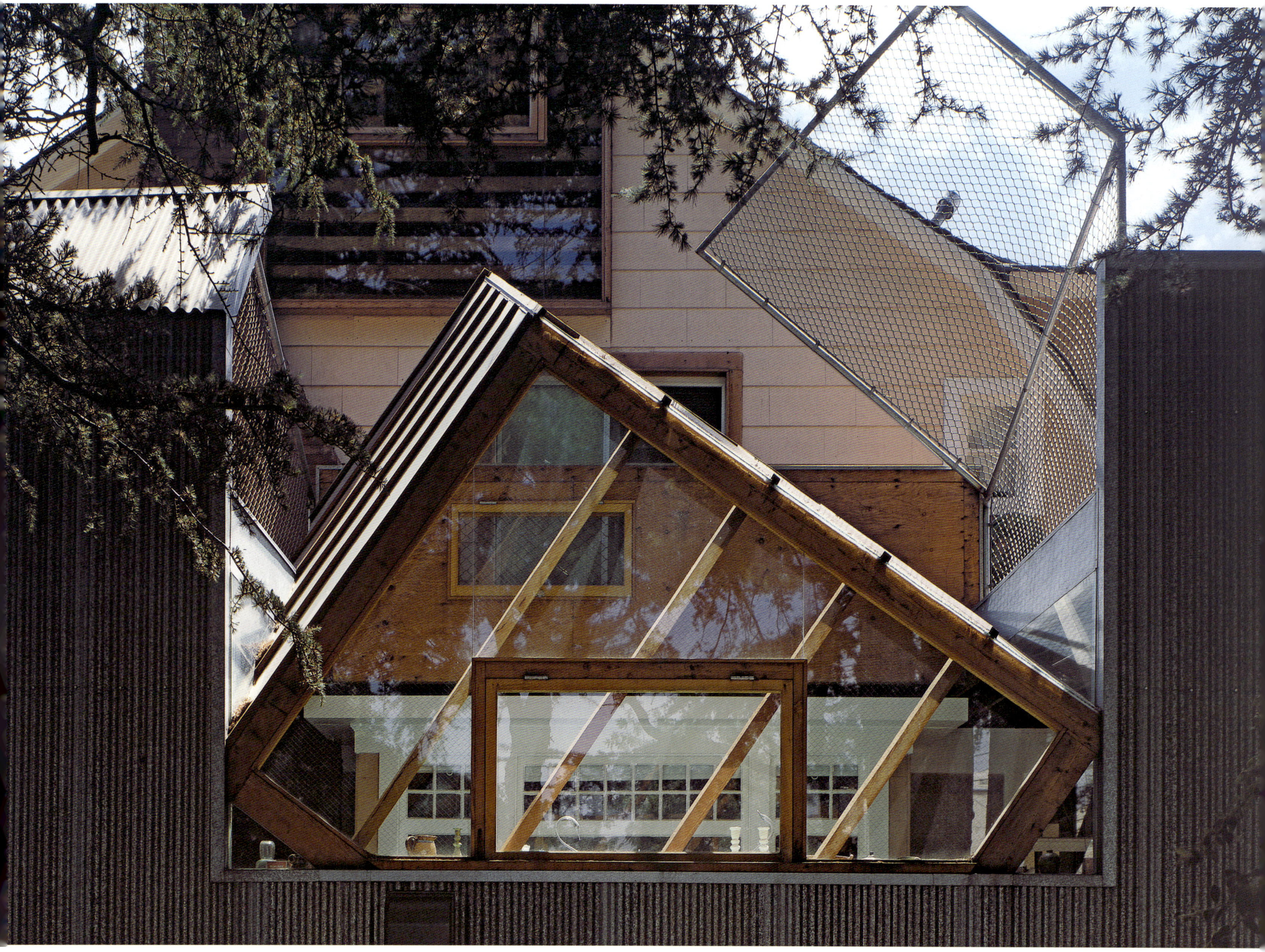

49

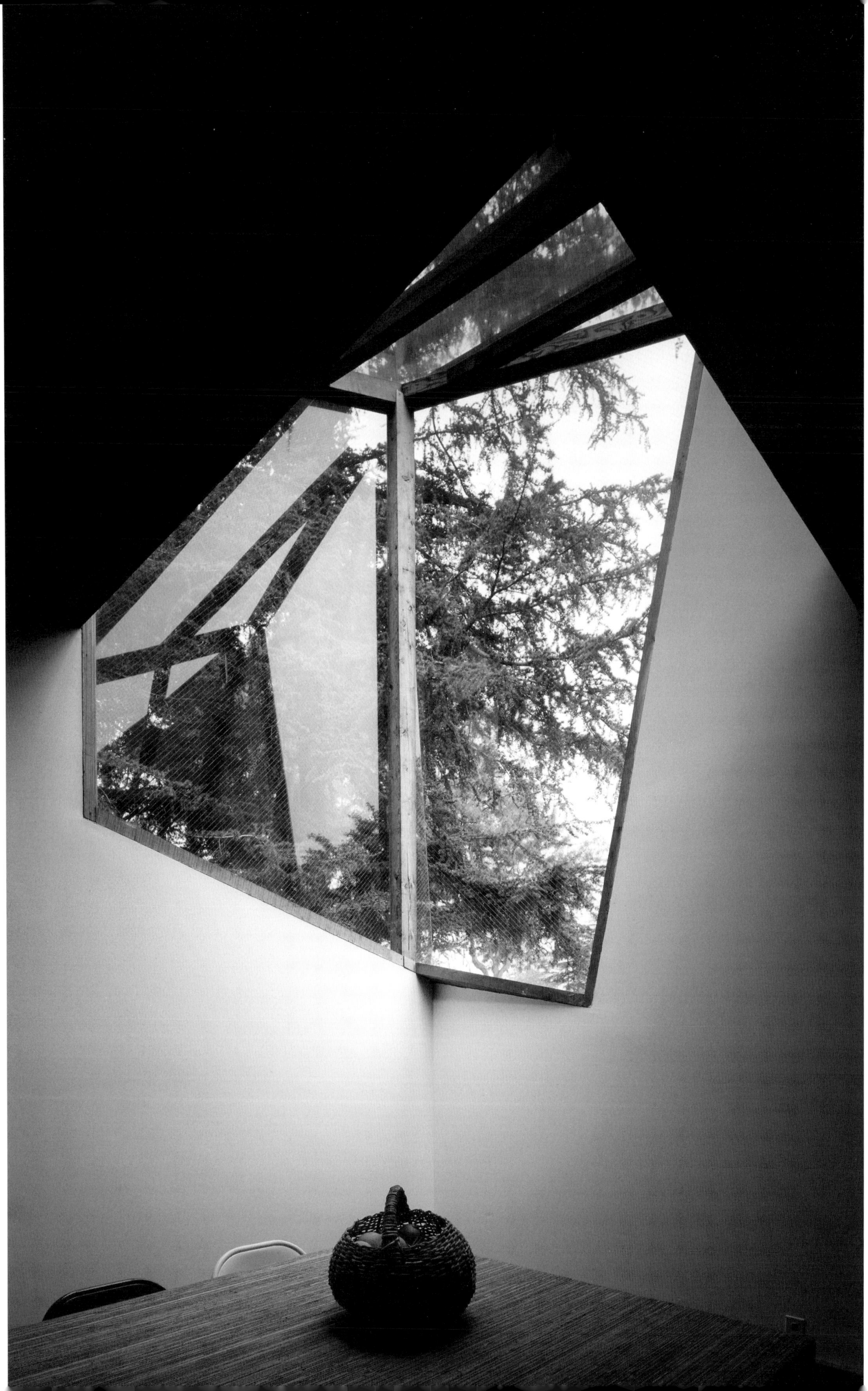

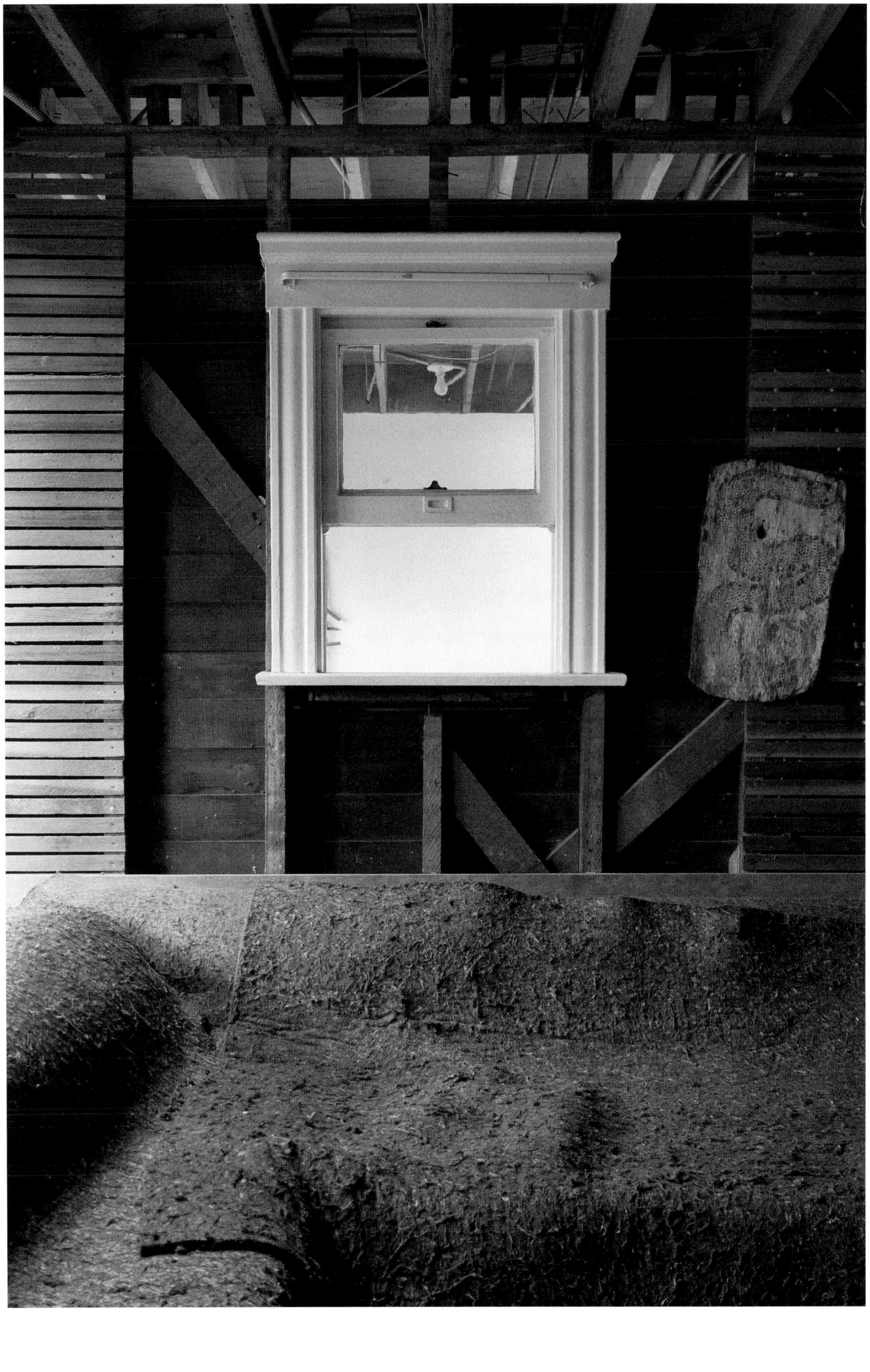

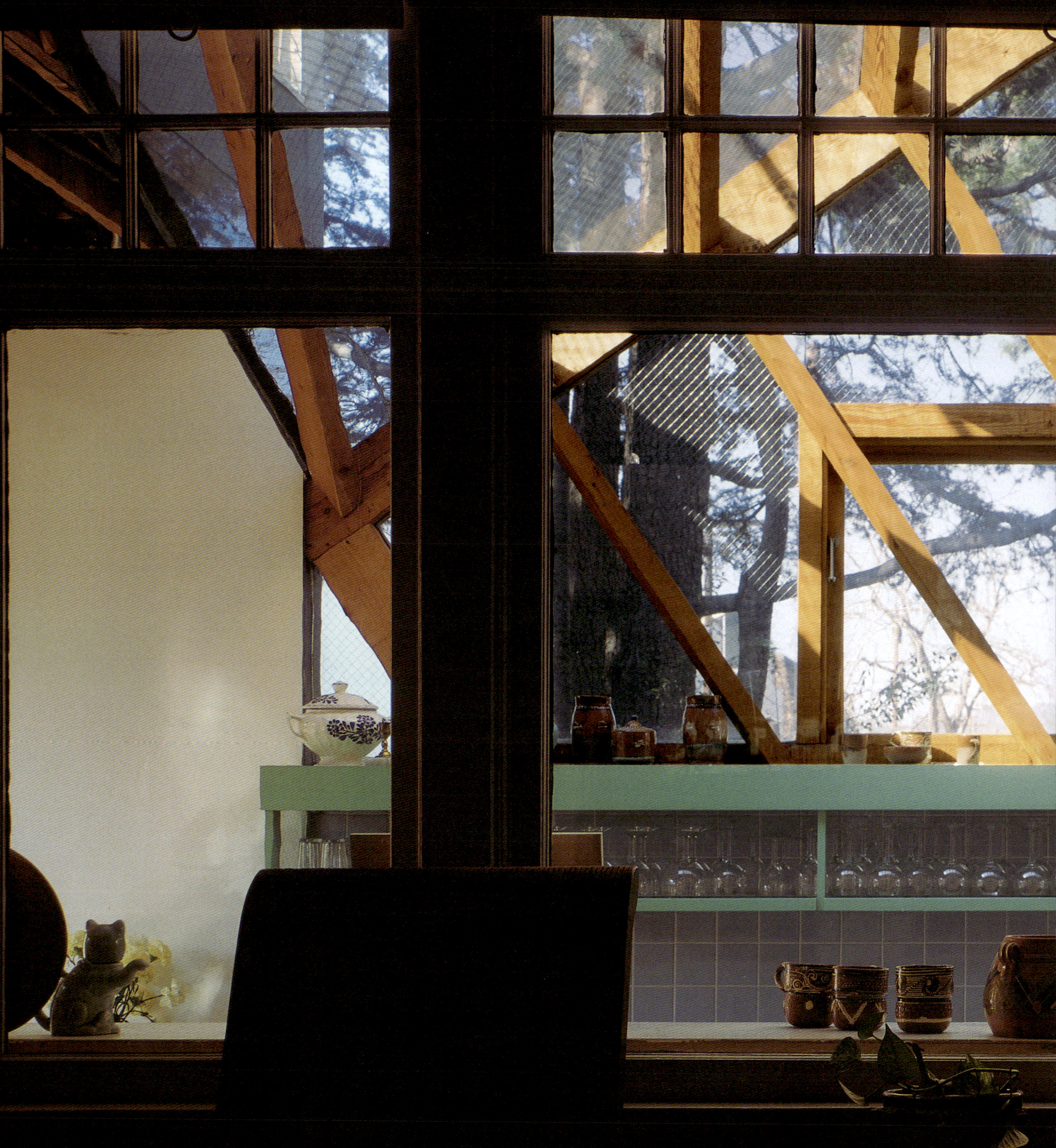

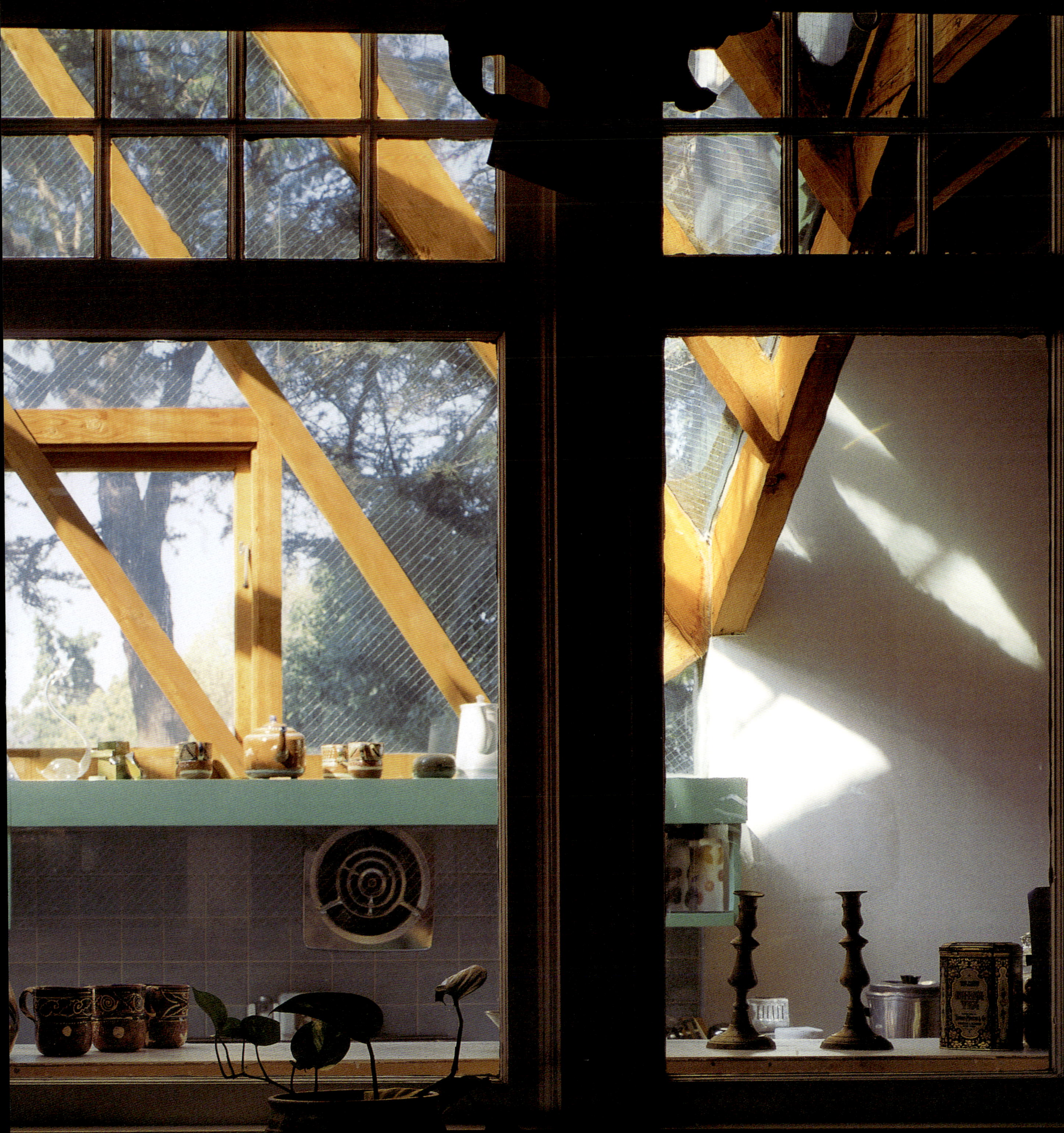

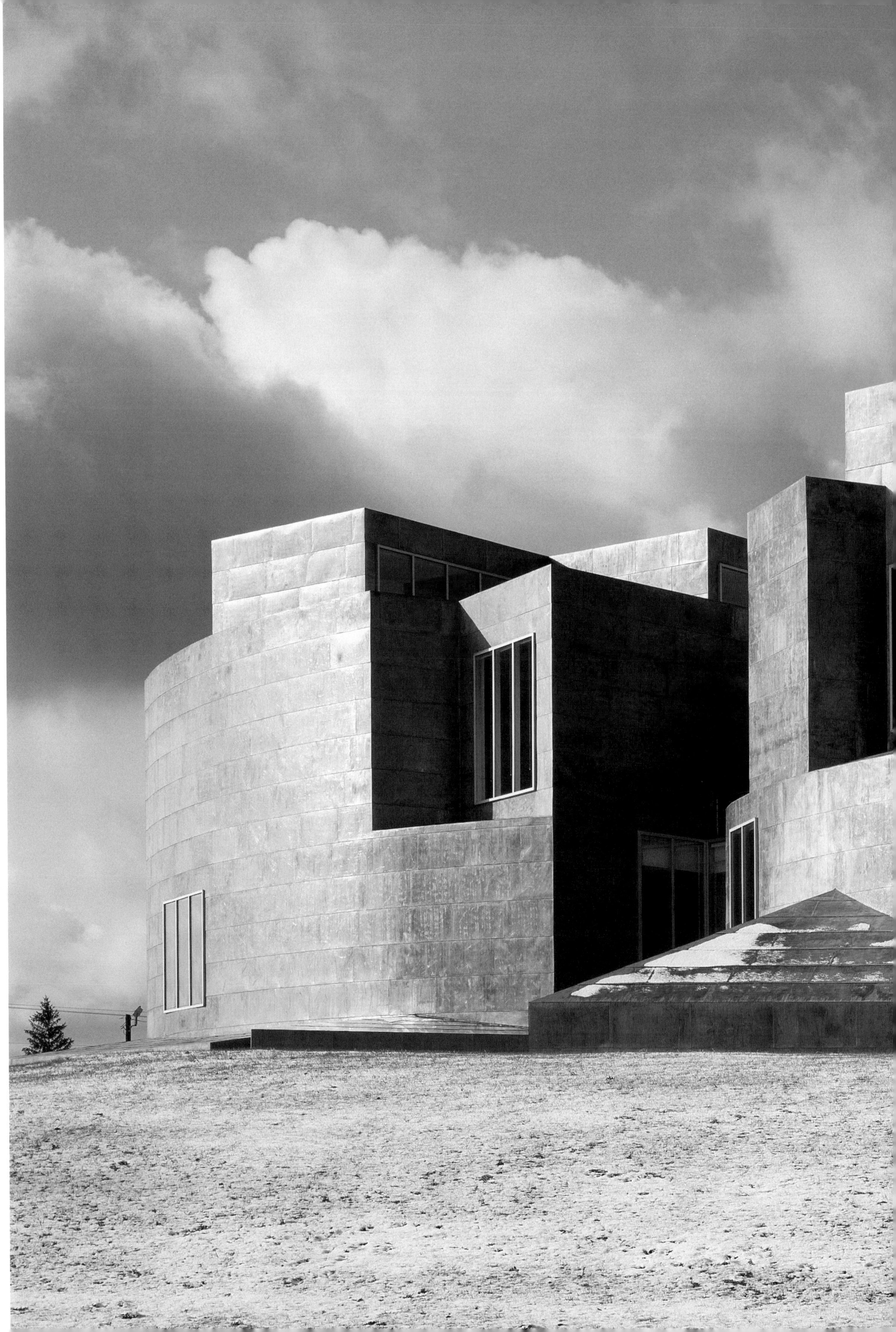

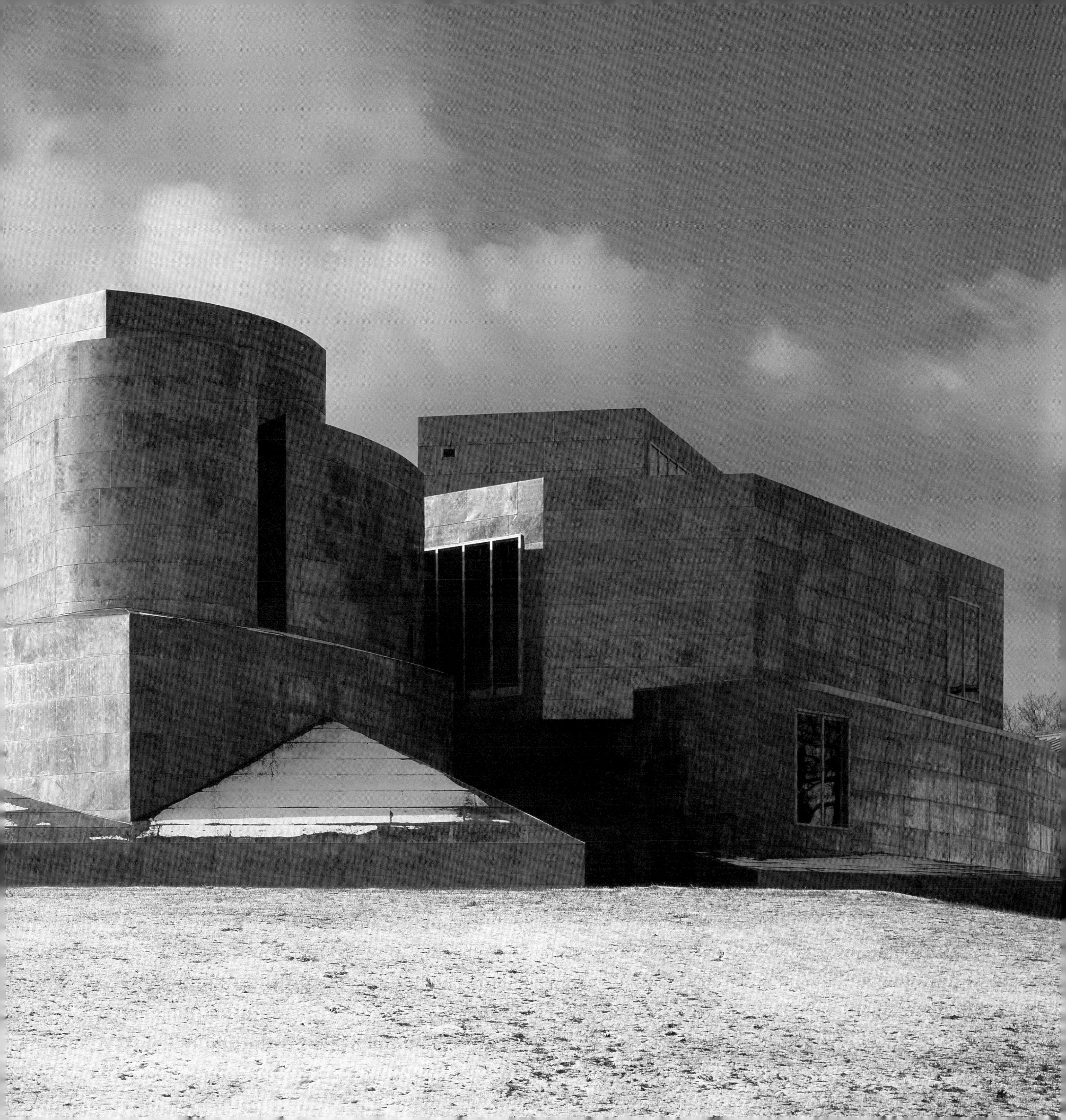

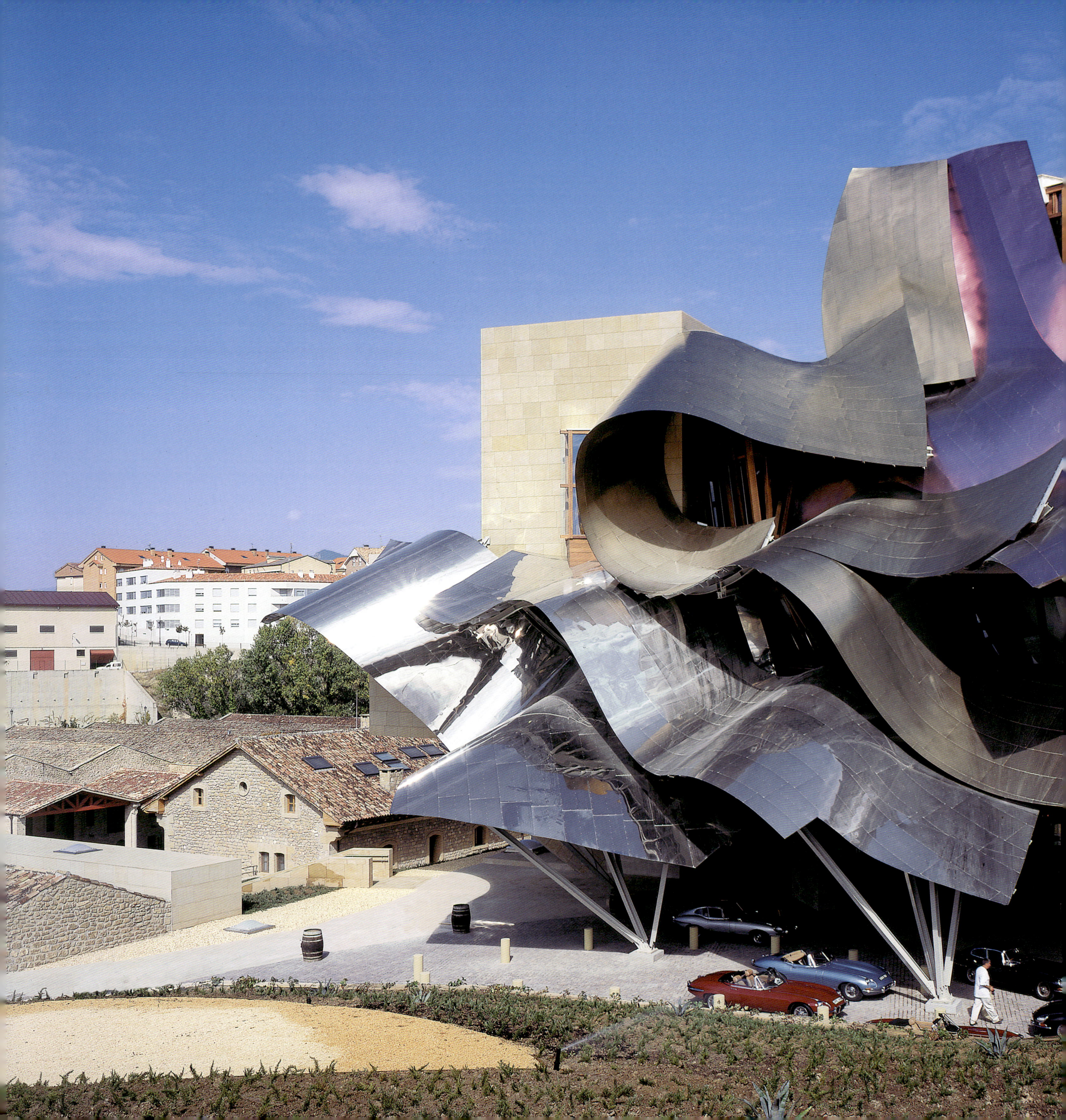

HOTEL AT MARQUES DE RISCAL 1998–2006

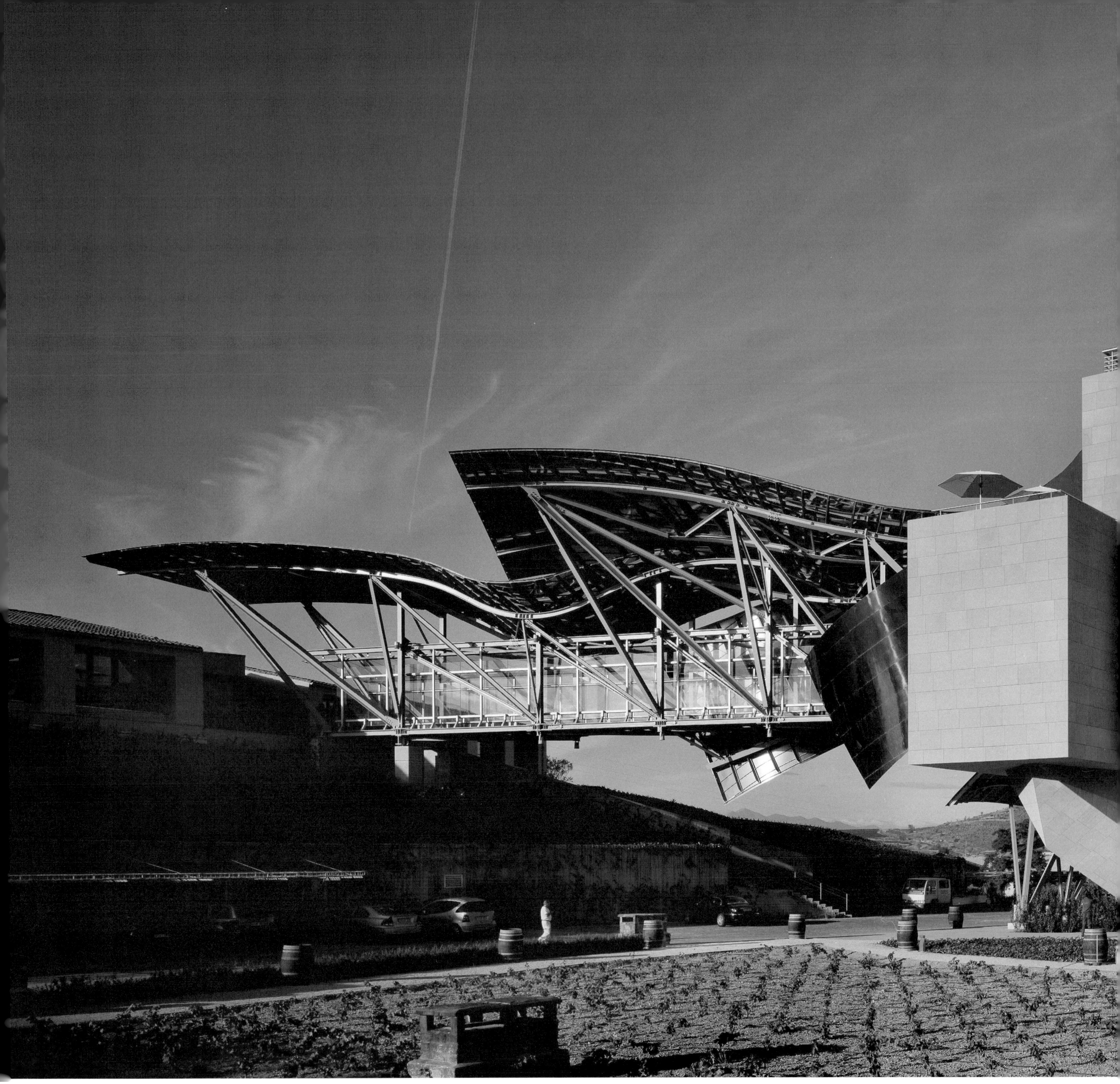

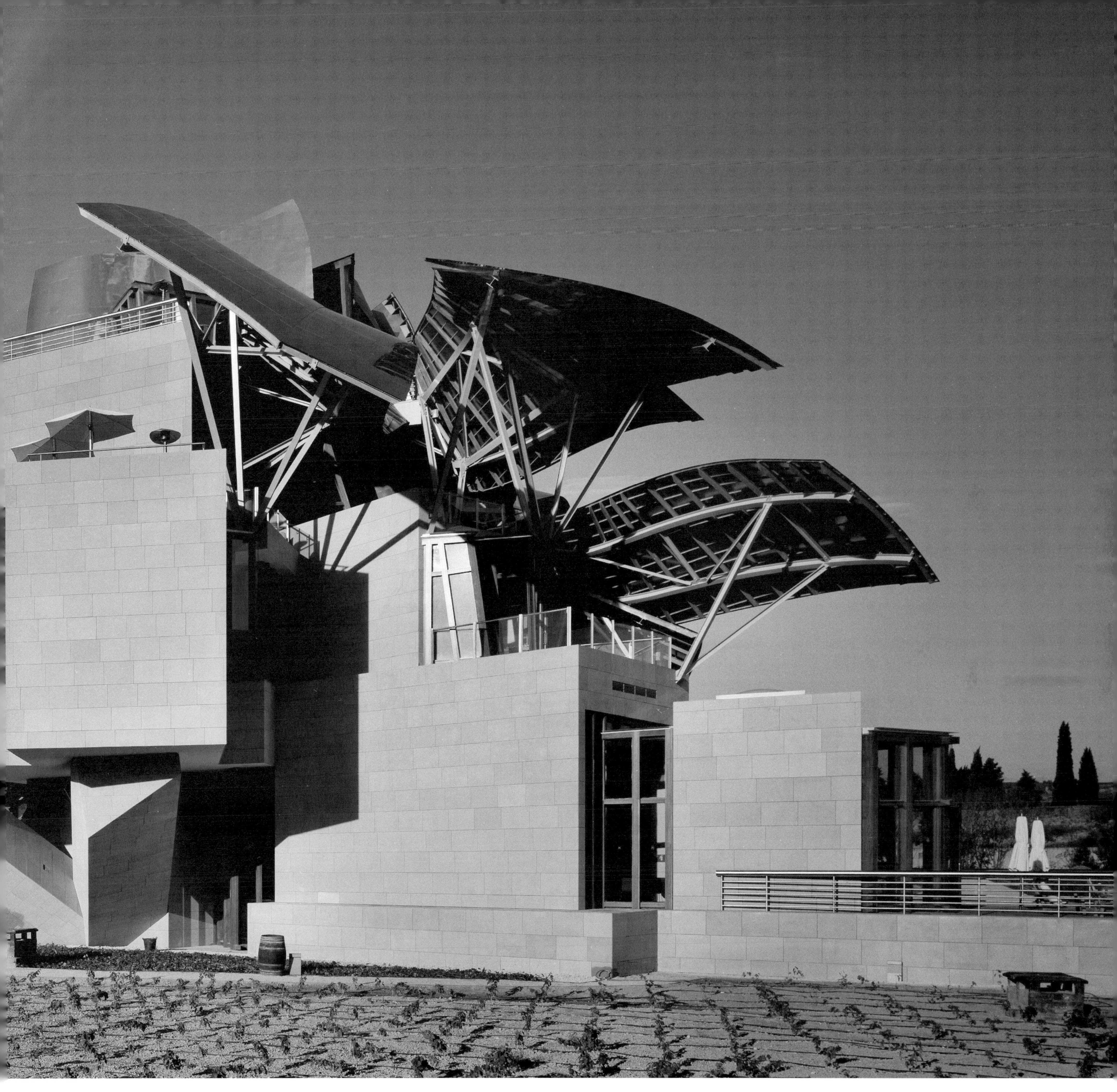

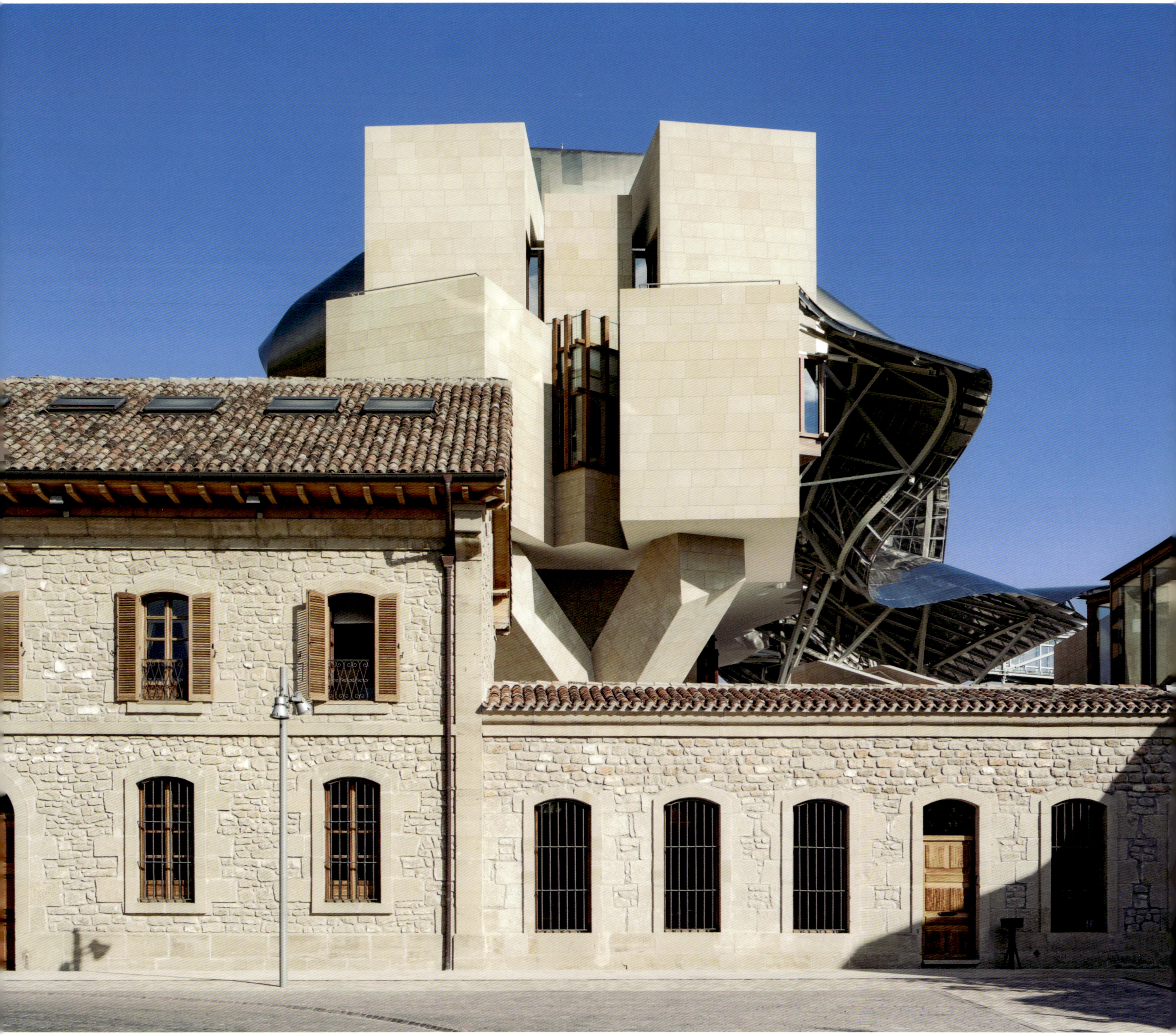

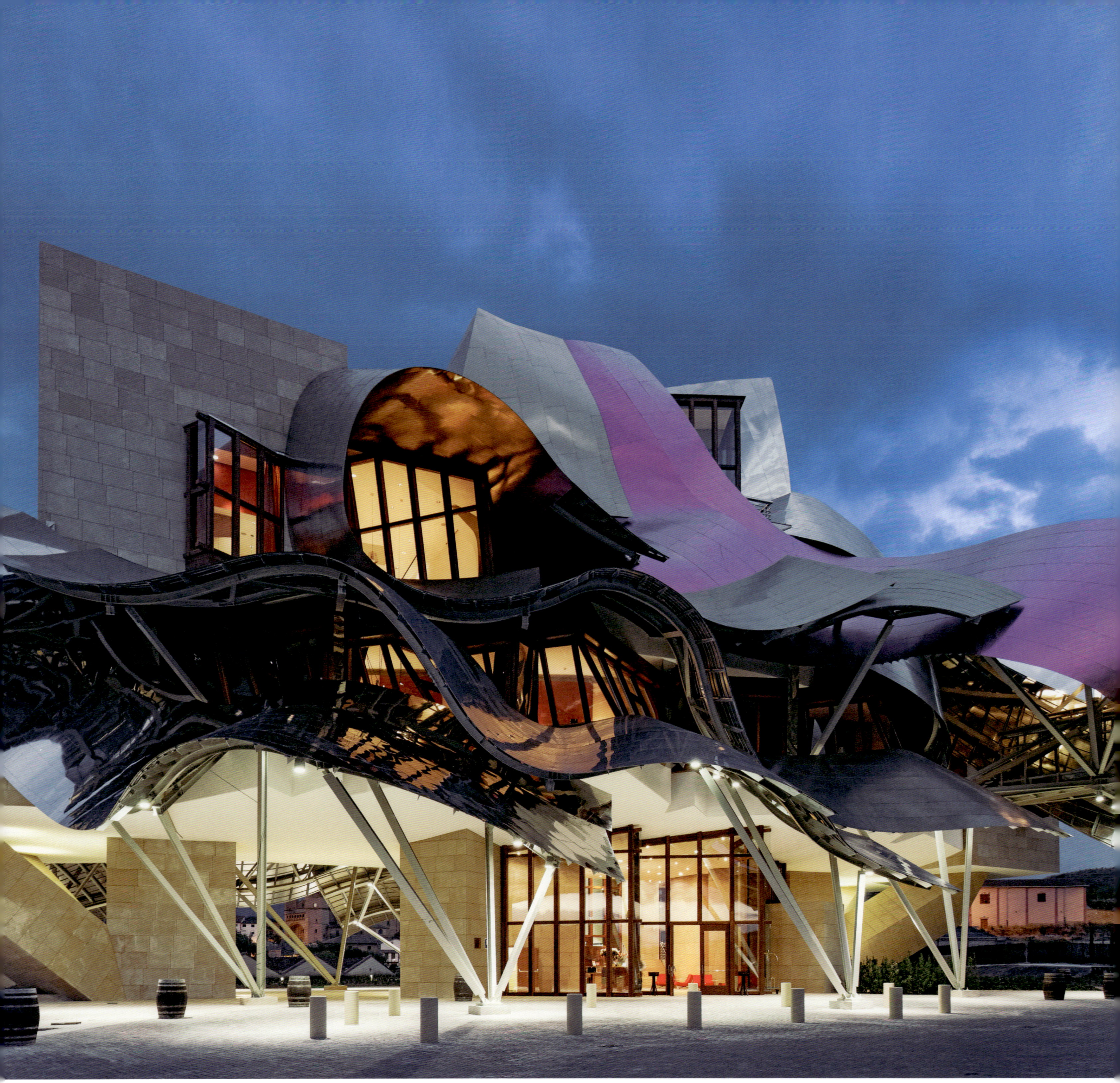

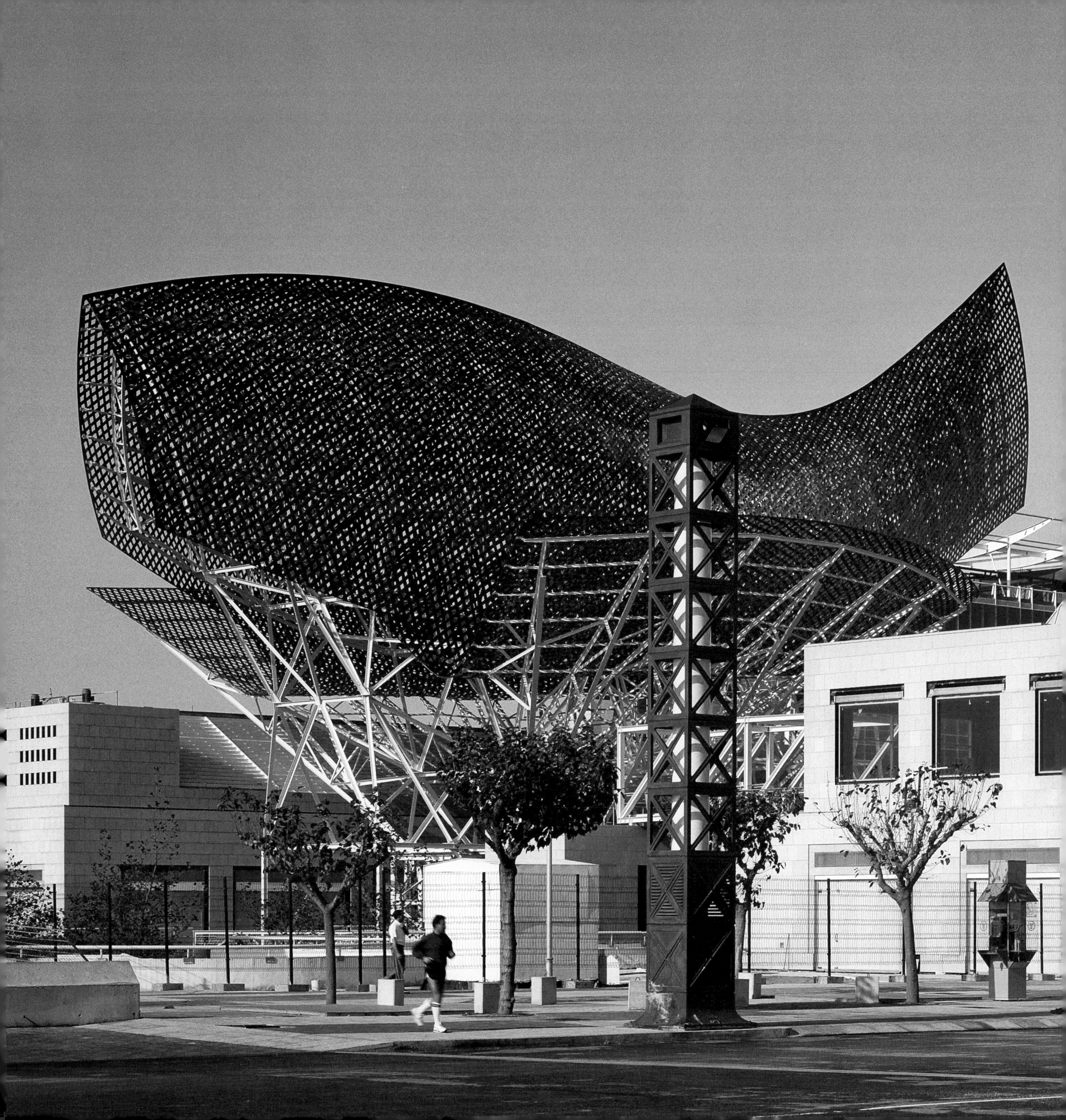

VILA OLÍMPICA 1989-1992

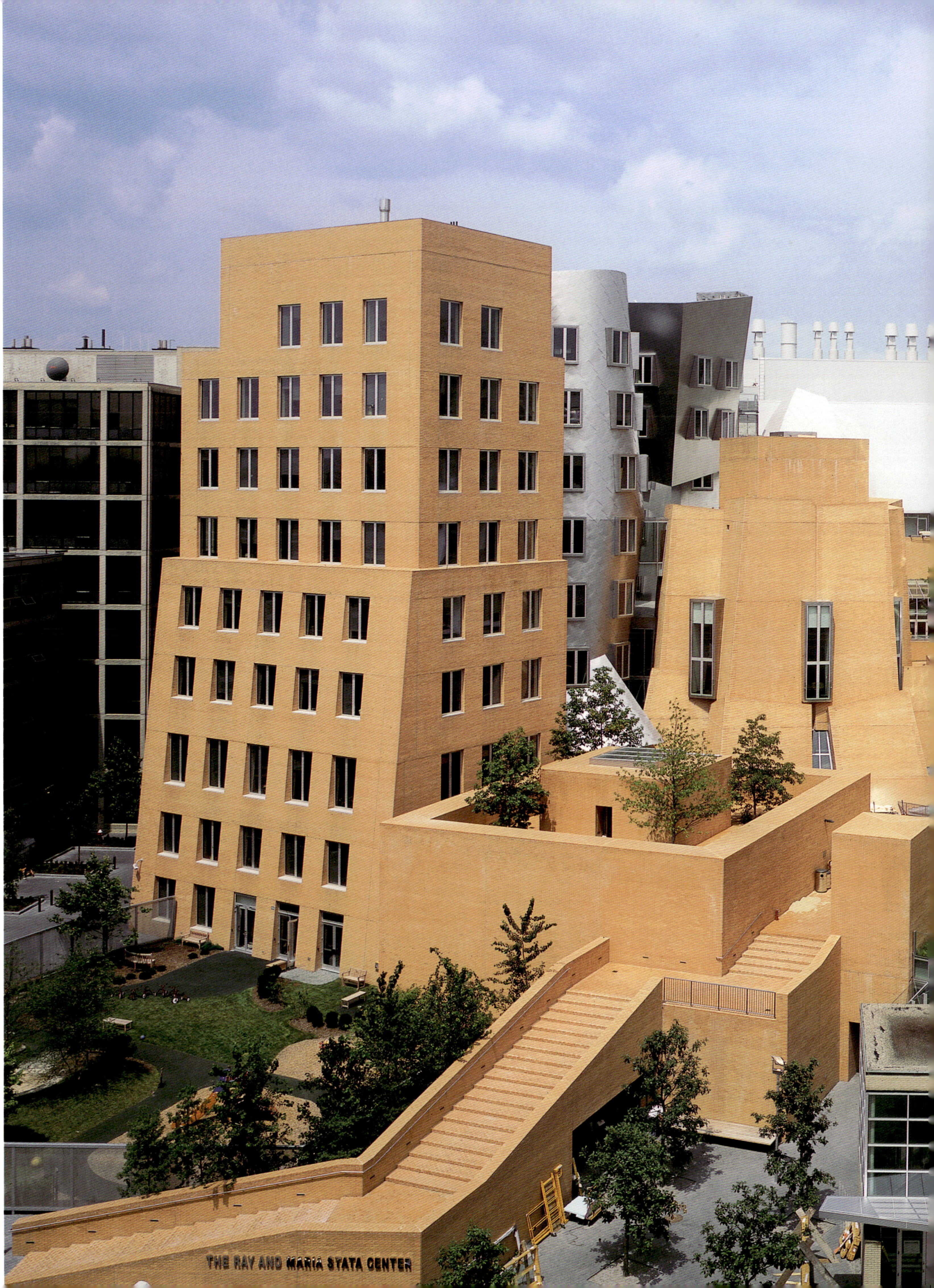
THE RAY AND MARIA STATA CENTER

RAY AND MARIA STATA CENTER FOR COMPUTER, INFORMATION AND INTELLIGENCE SCIENCES, MASSACHUSETTS INSTITUTE OF TECHNOLOGY 1998-2004

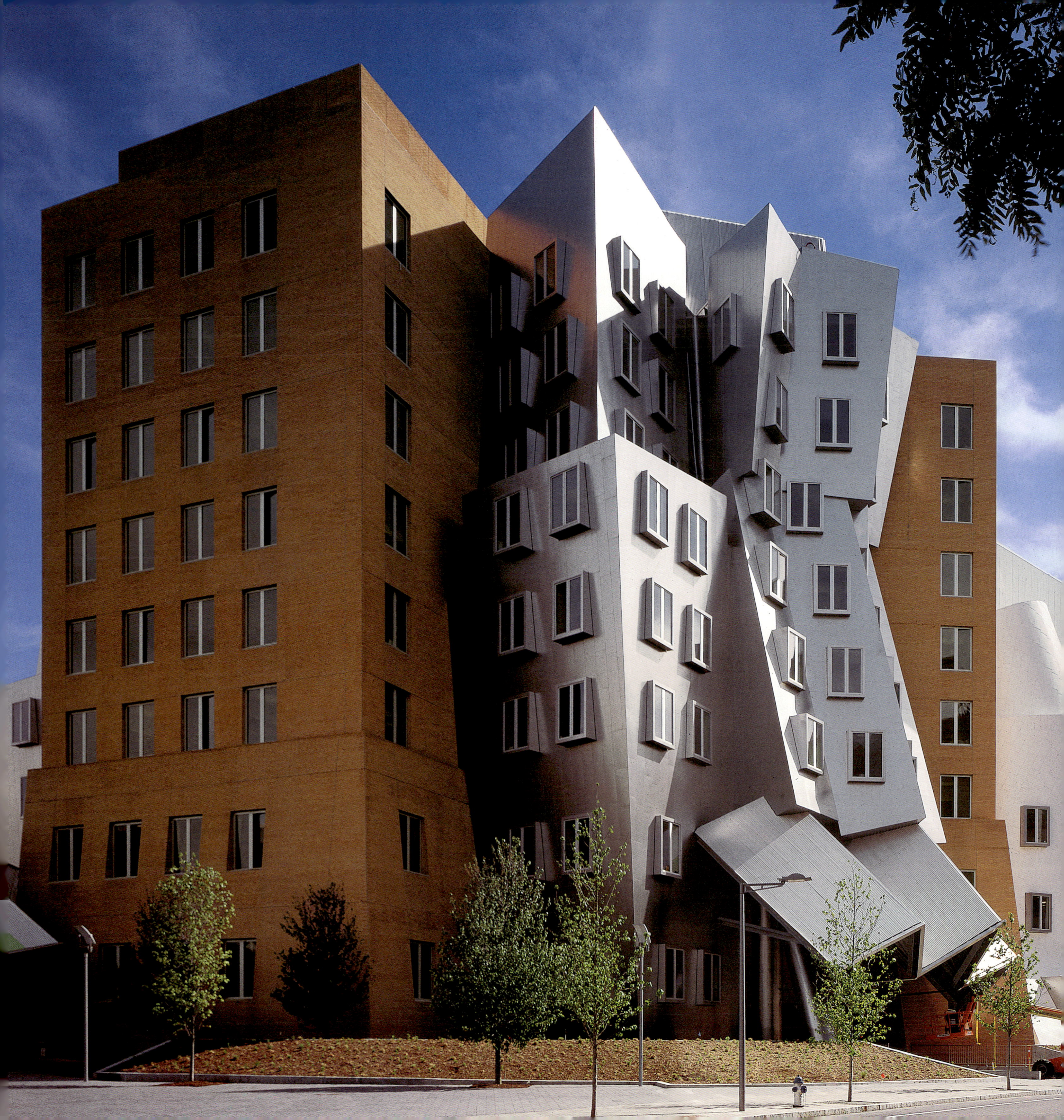

67

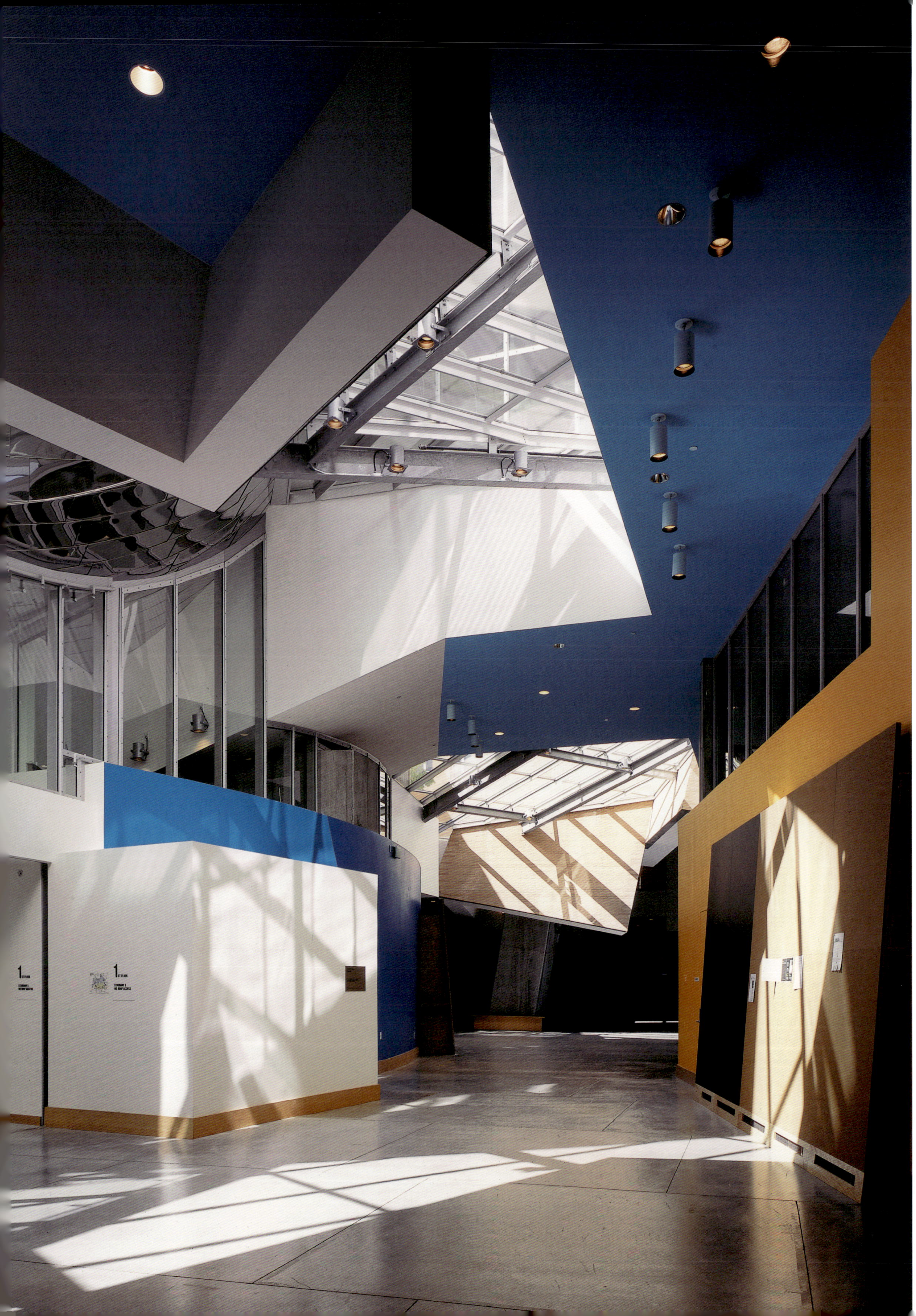

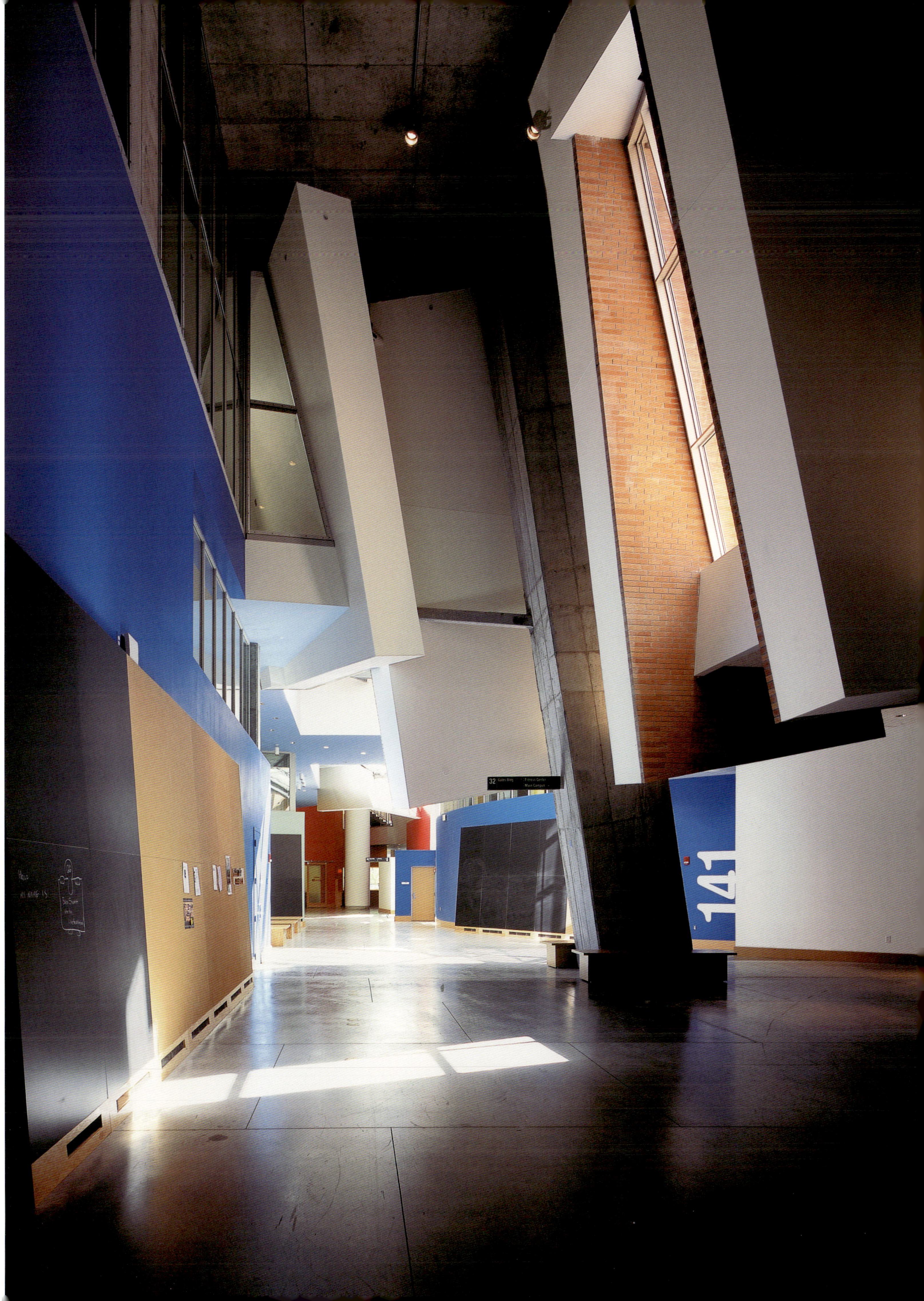
141

EXPERIENCE MUSIC PROJECT   1995–2000

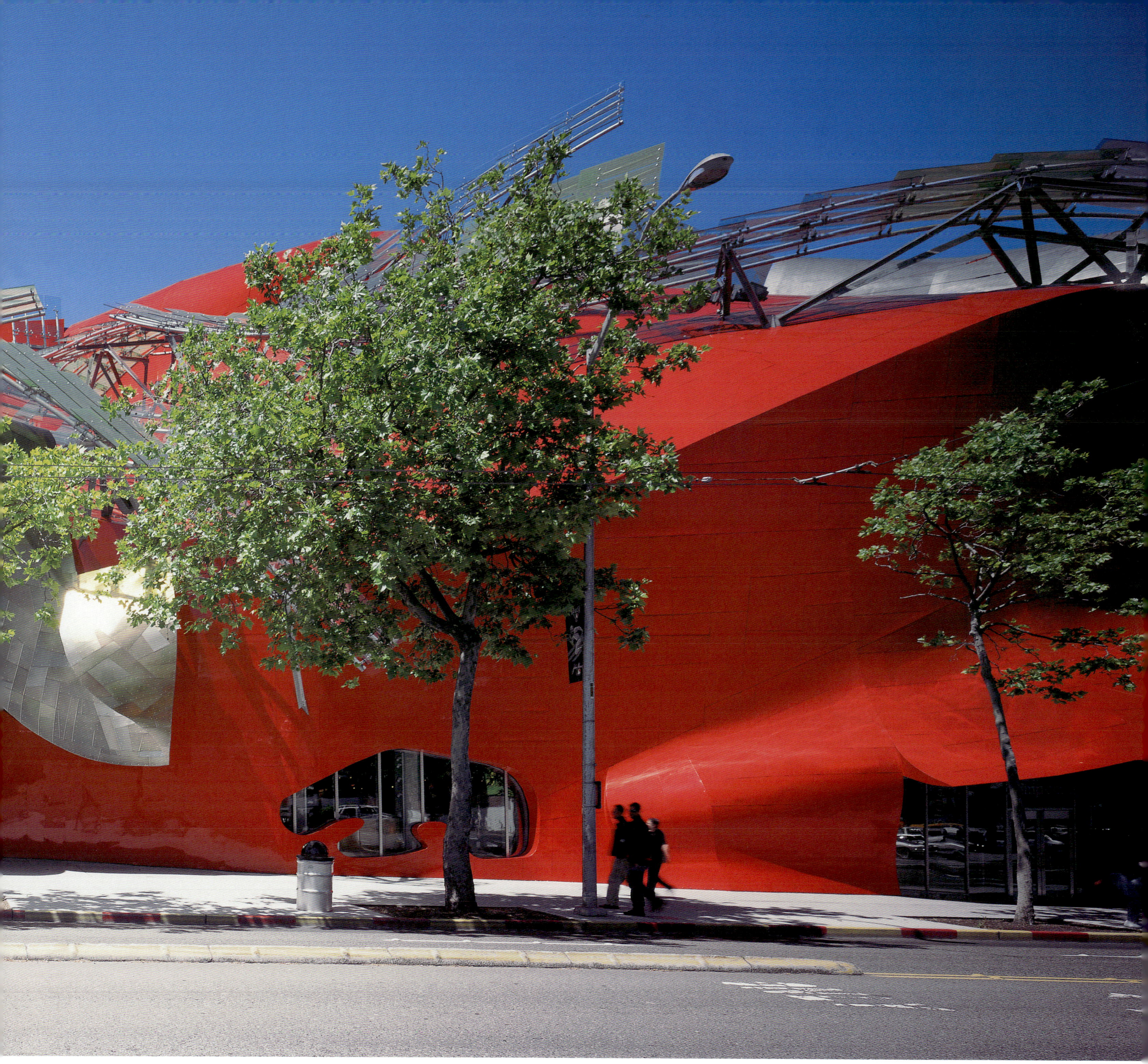

72

73

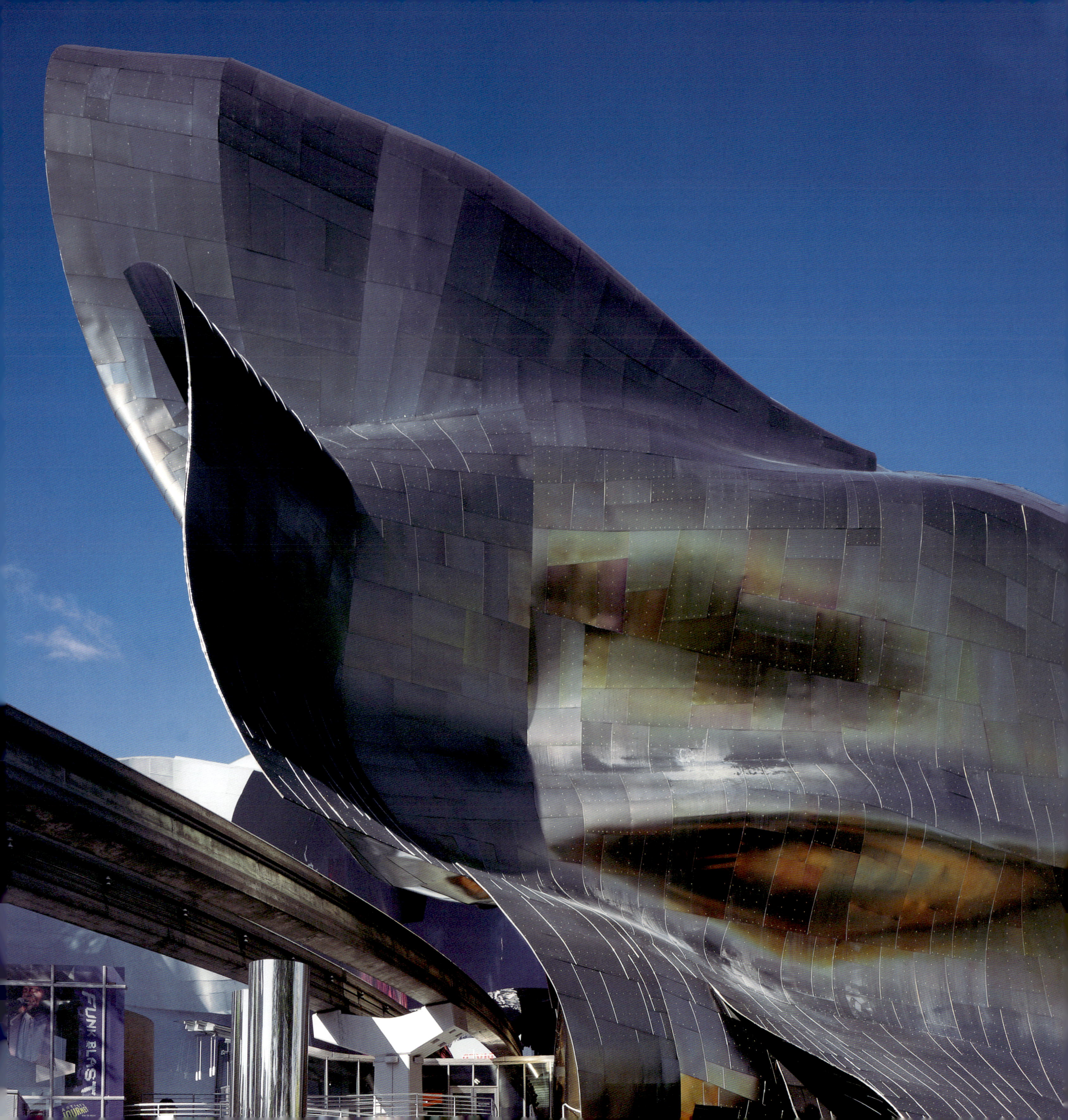
FUNK BLAST

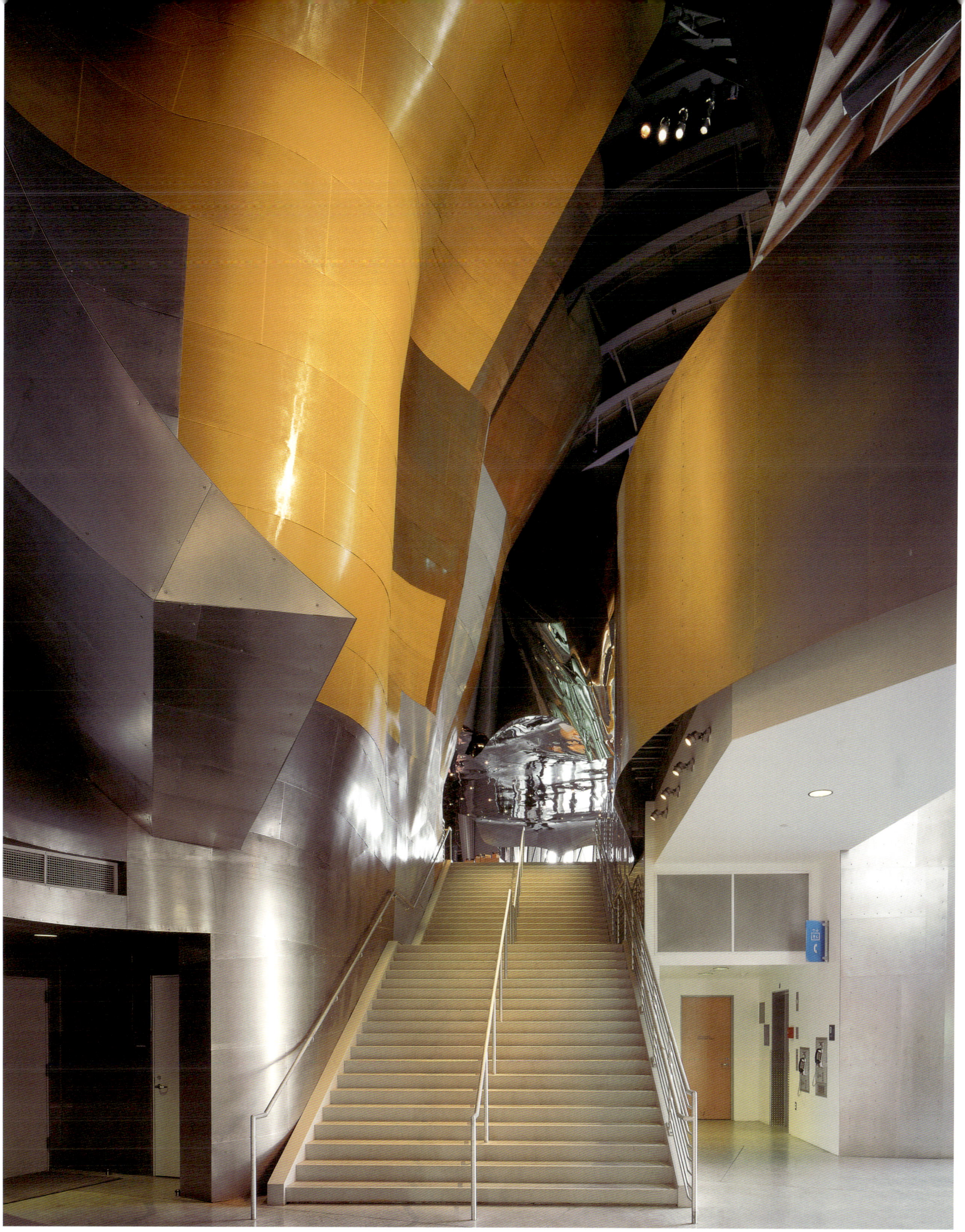

LOYOLA LAW SCHOOL, LOYOLA MARYMOUNT UNIVERSITY 1978-91

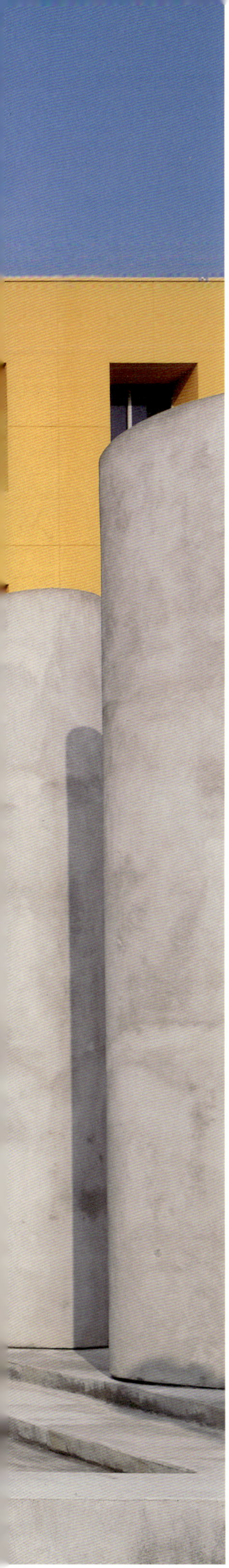

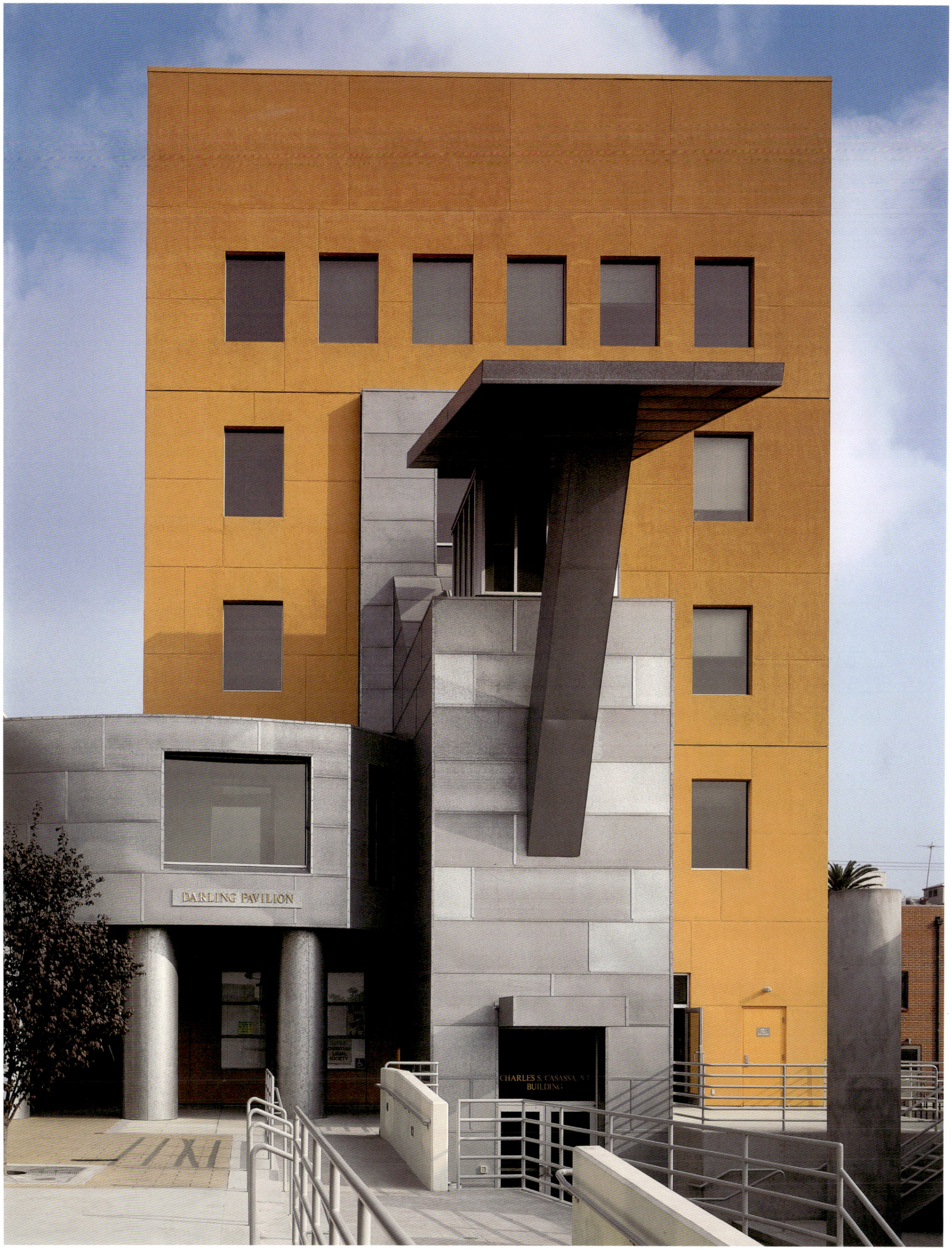
DARLING PAVILION

IOWA ADVANCED TECHNOLOGY LABORATORIES BUILDING   1987–92

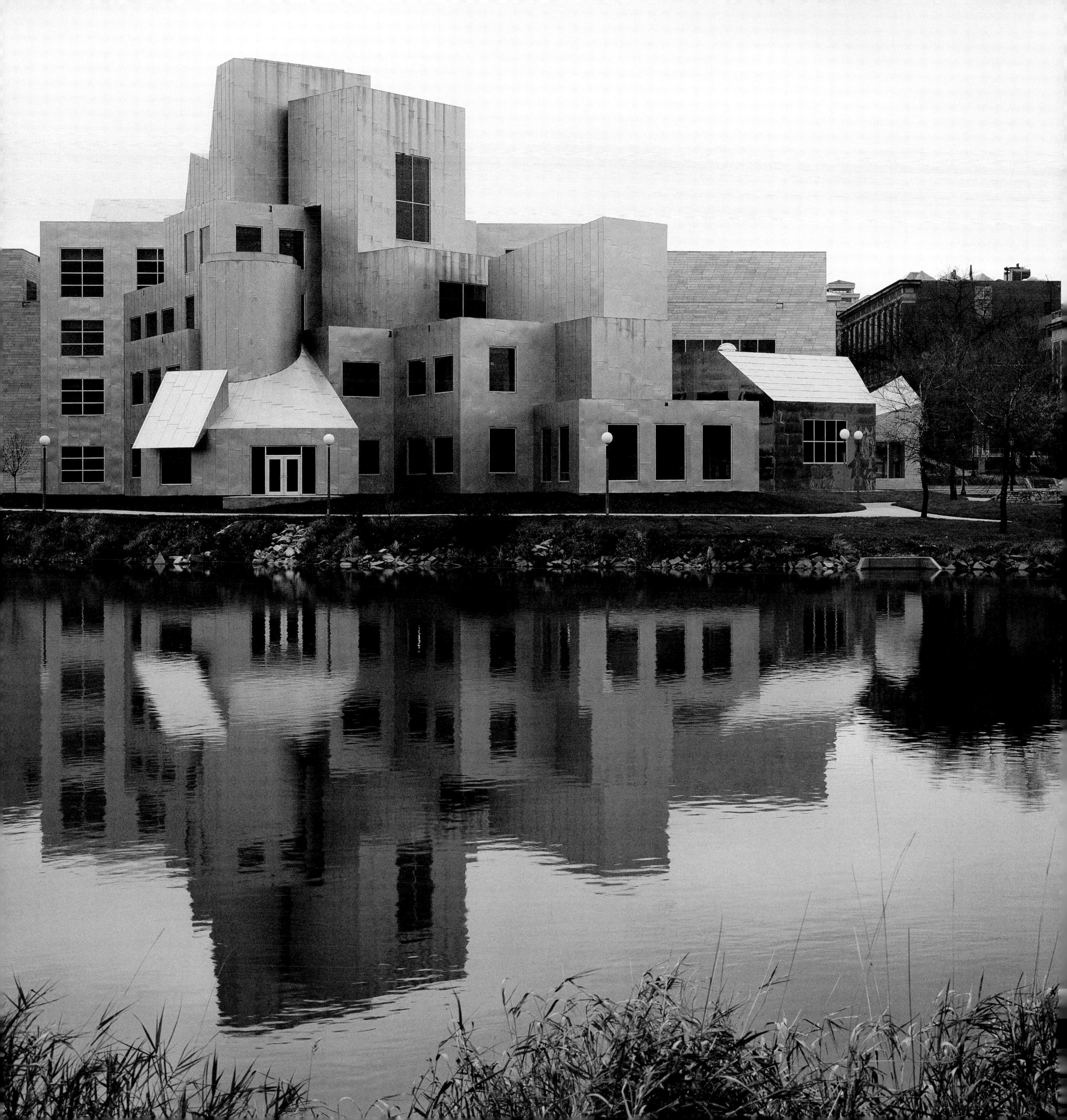

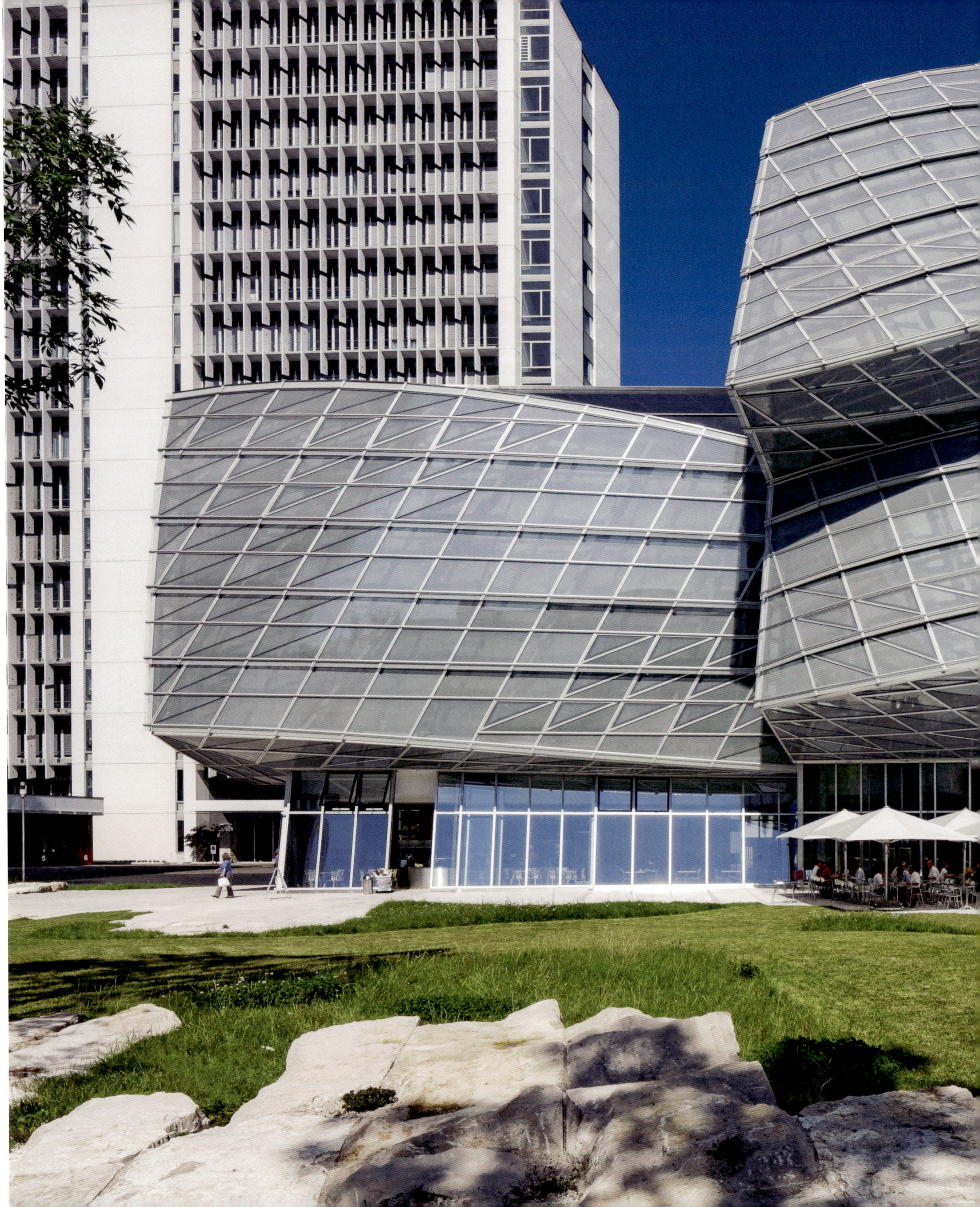

NOVARTIS CAMPUS GEHRY BUILDING 2003-09

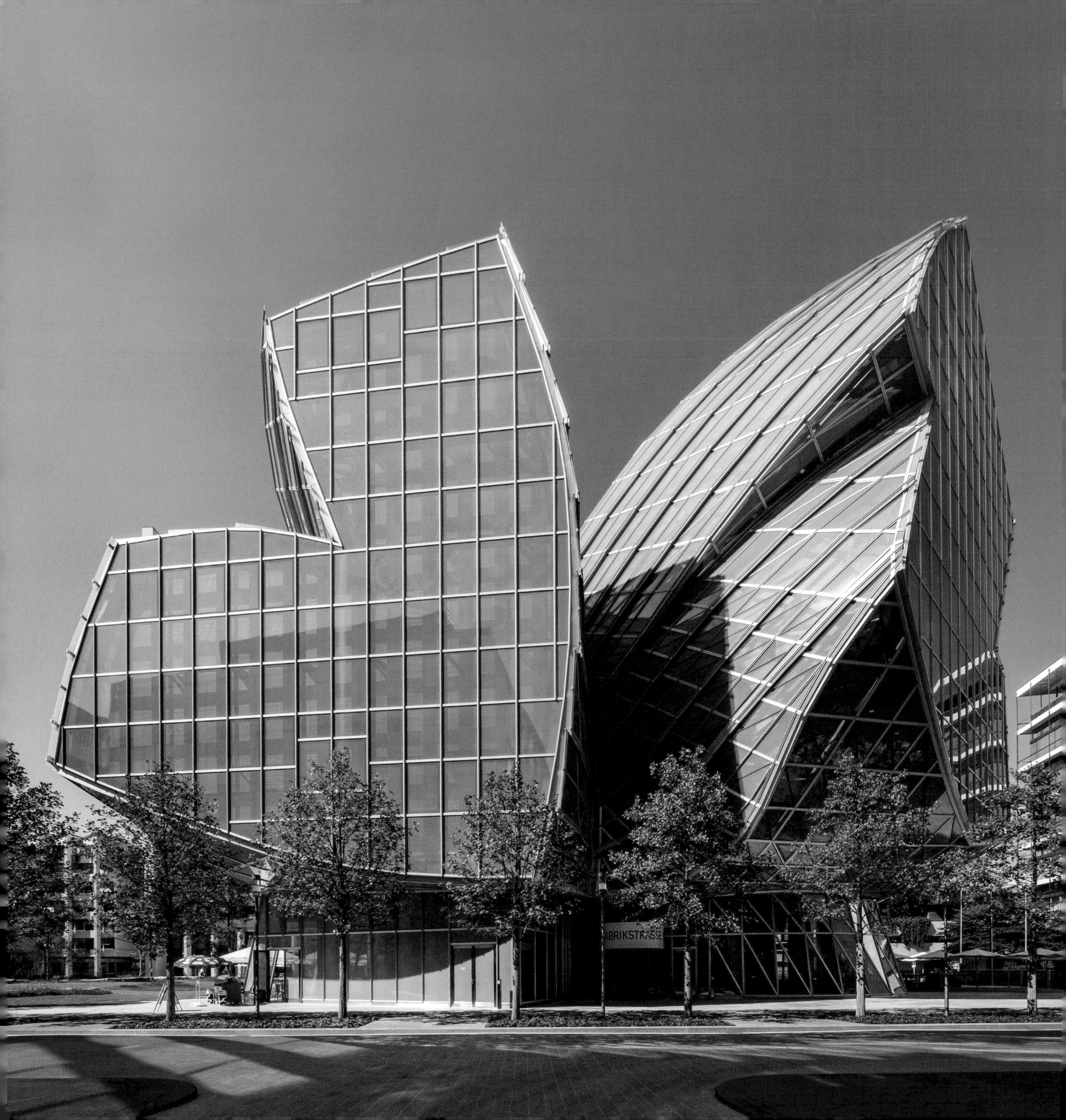
ABRIKSTRASSE

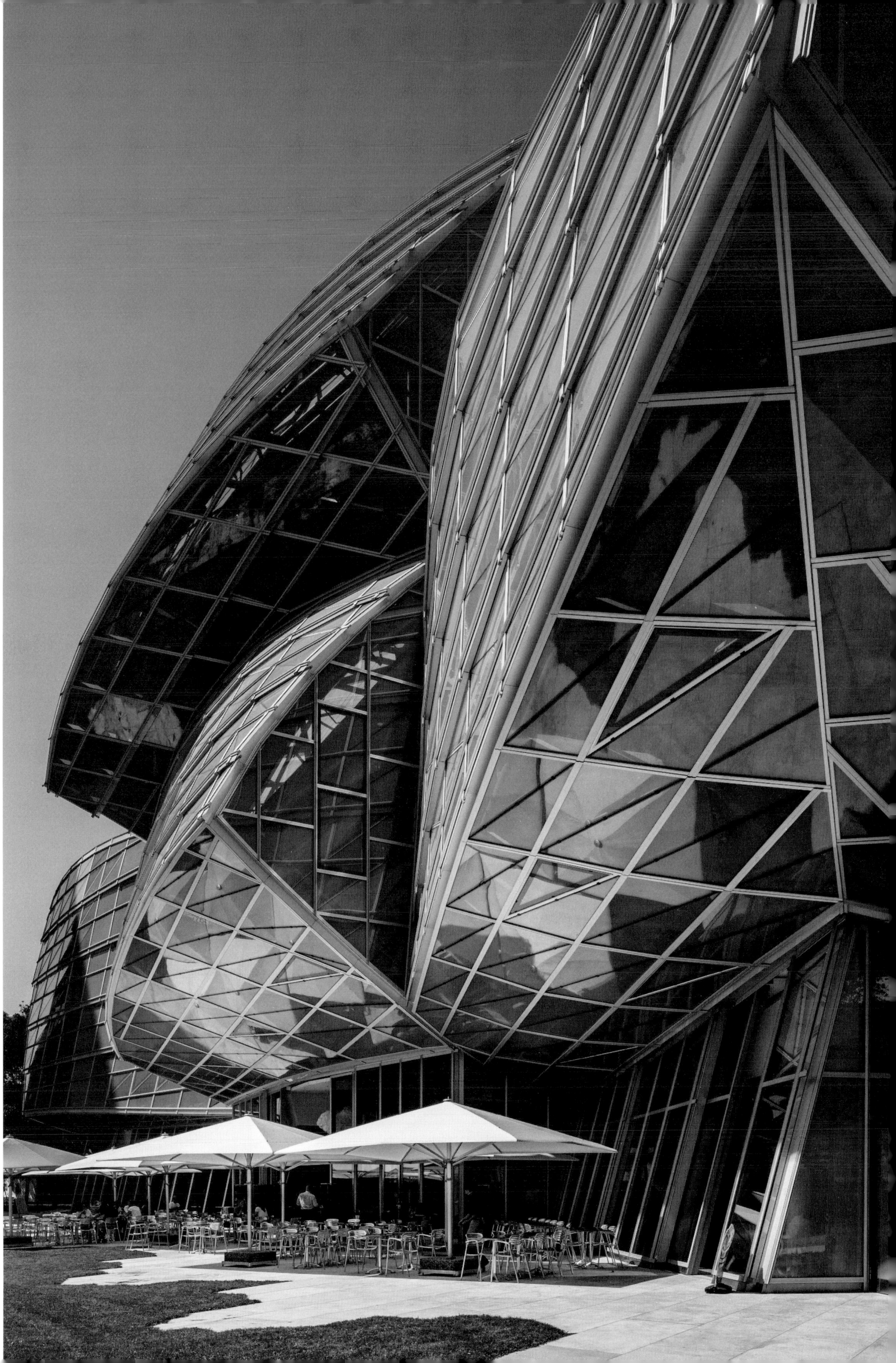

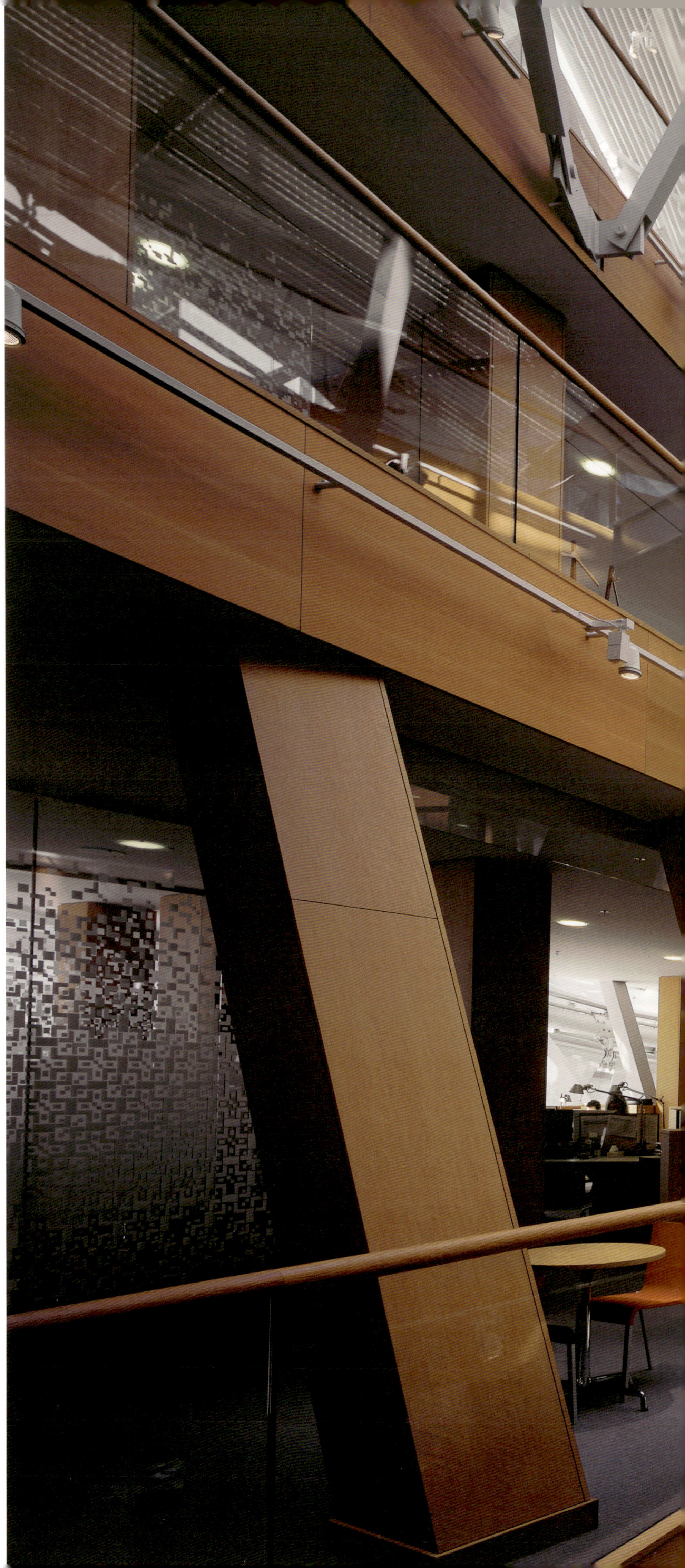

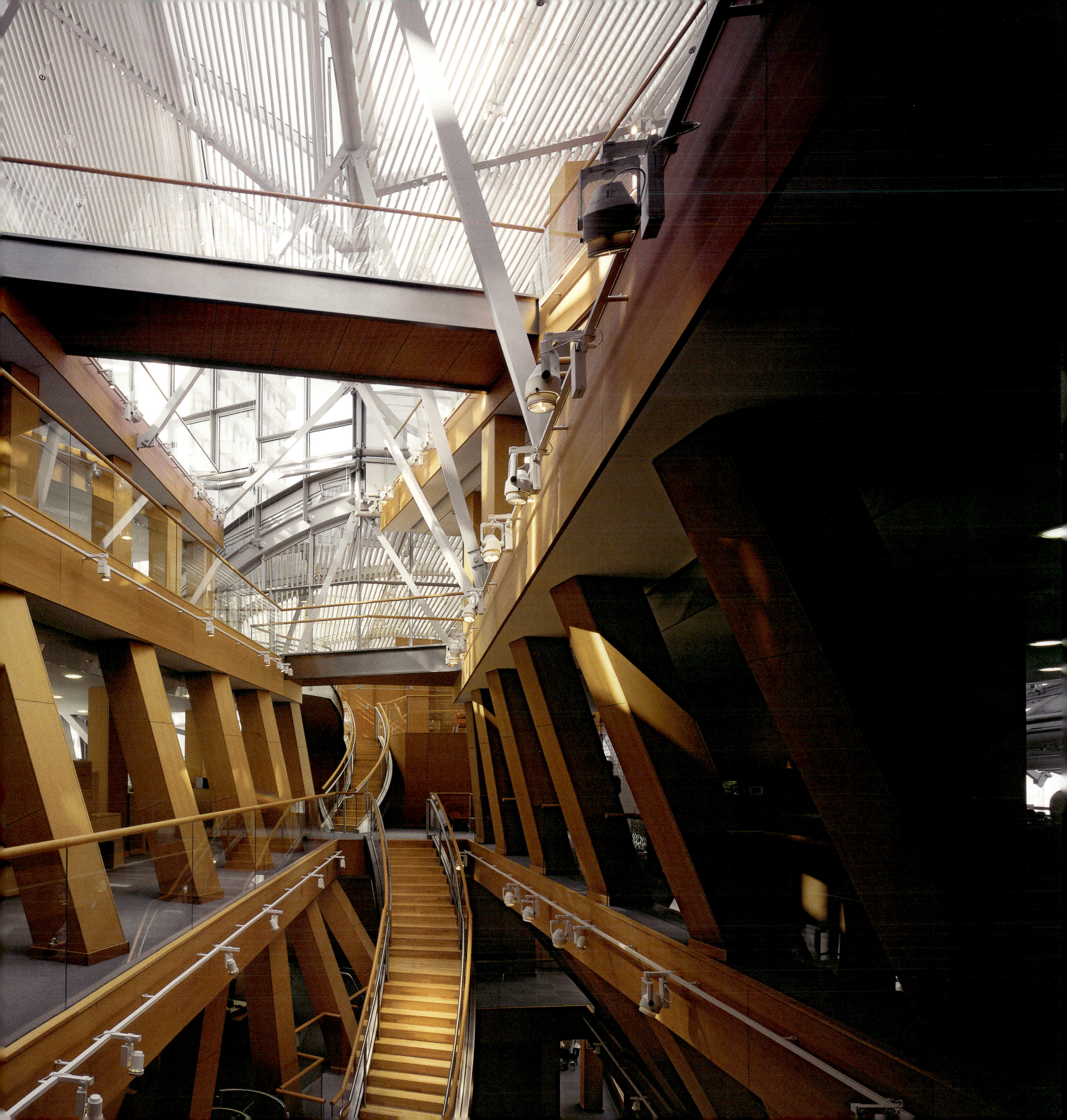

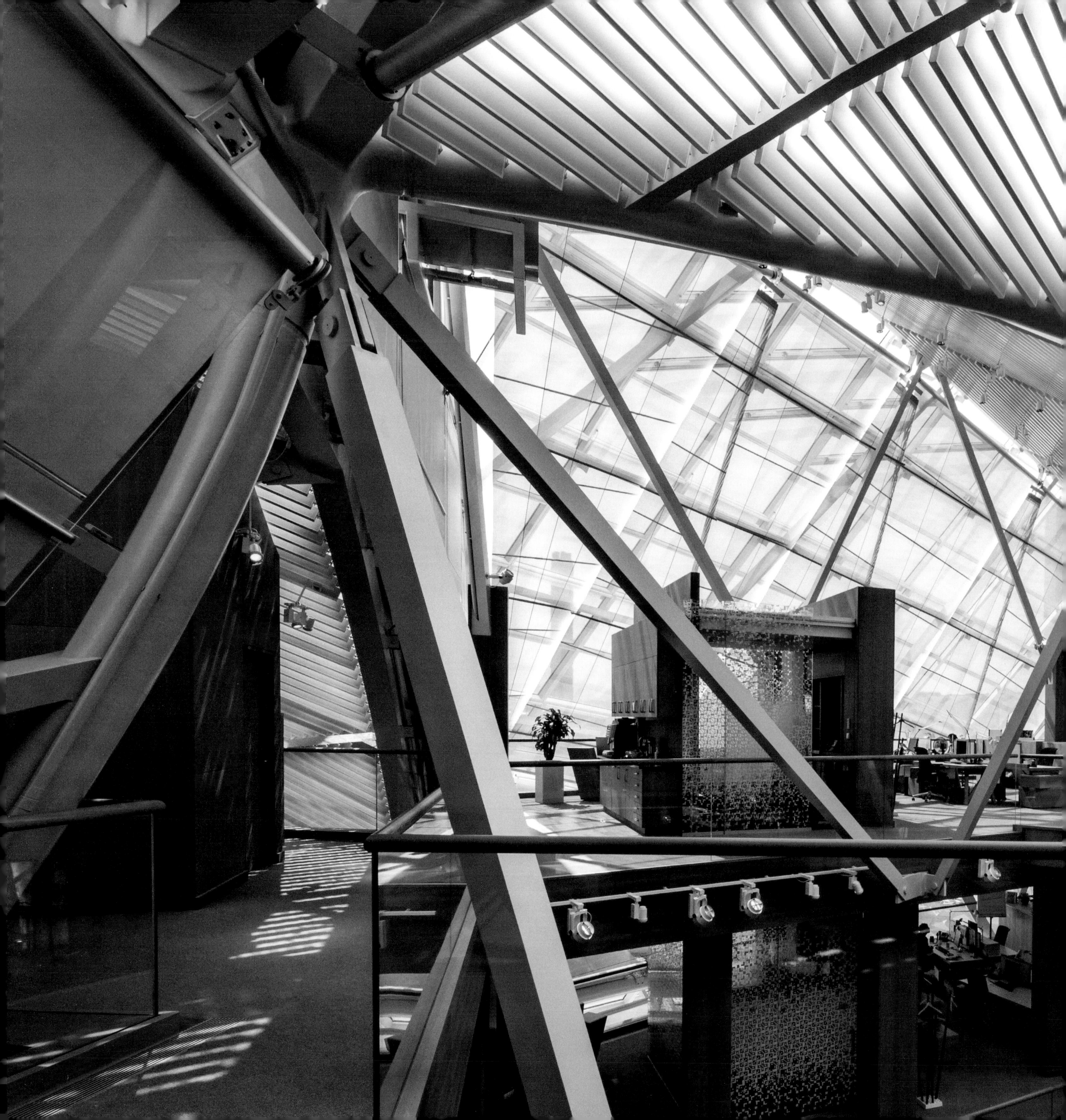

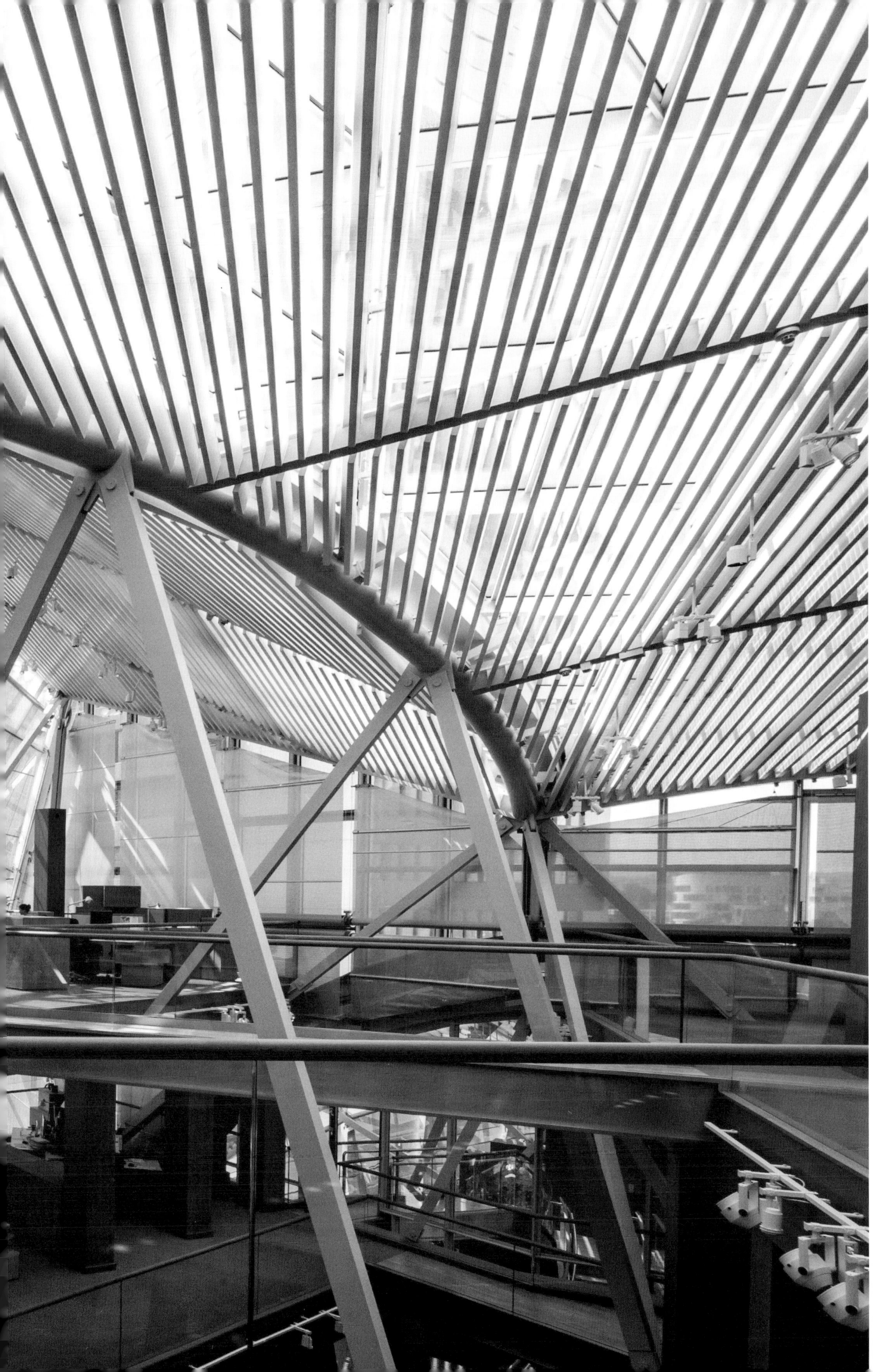

HERMAN MILLER, INC., WESTERN REGION MANUFACTURING & DISTRIBUTION FACILITY   1987-89

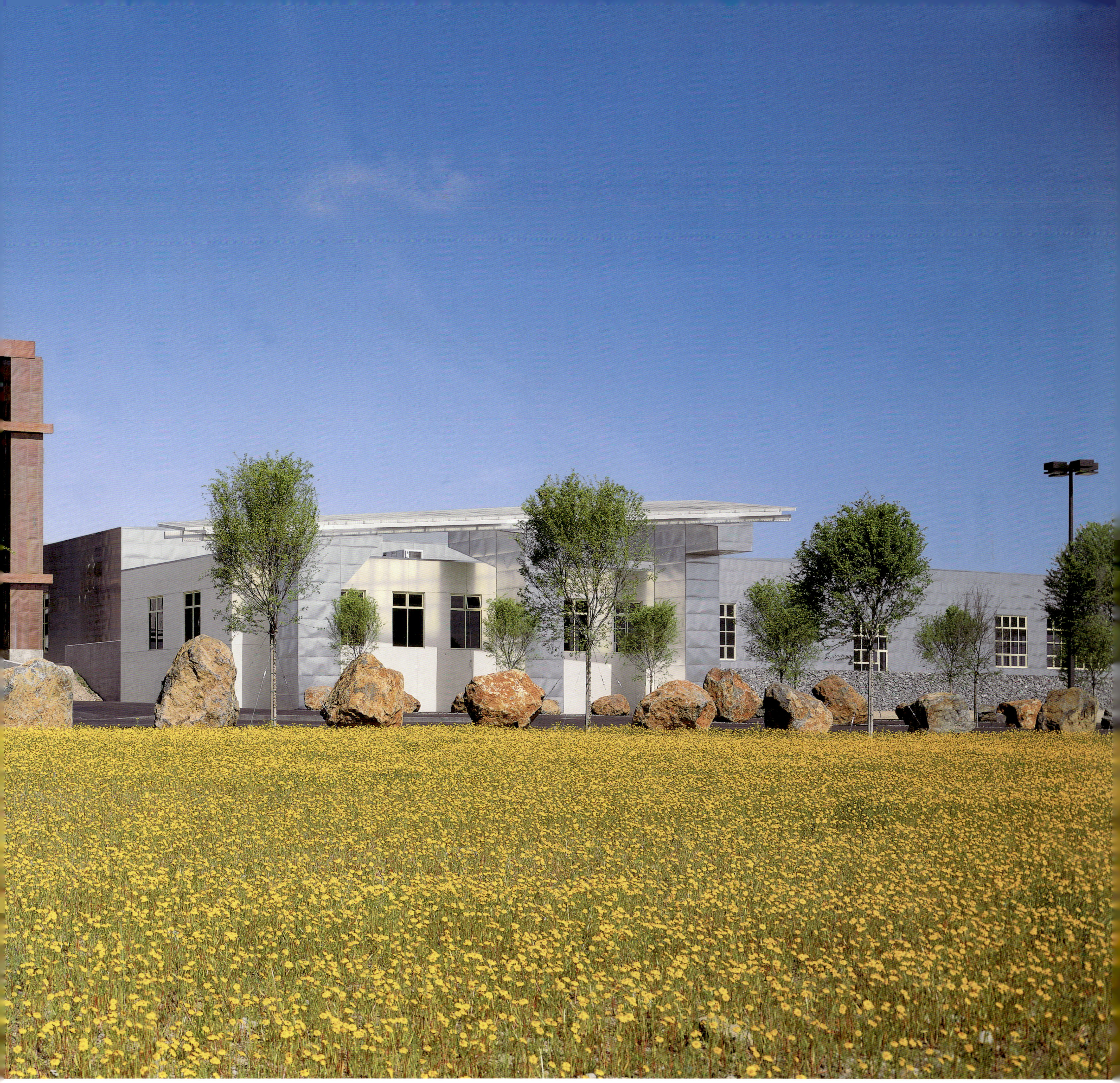

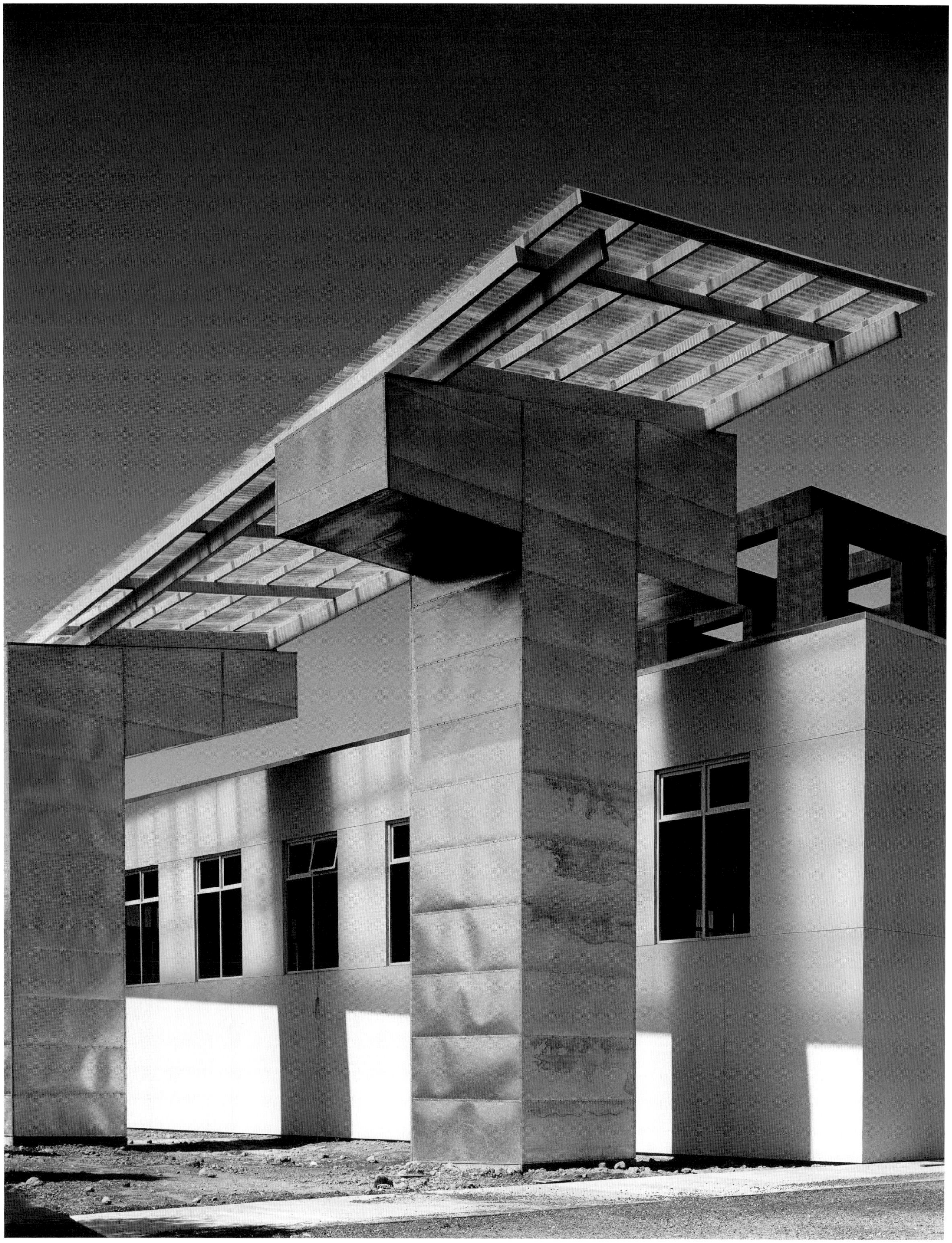

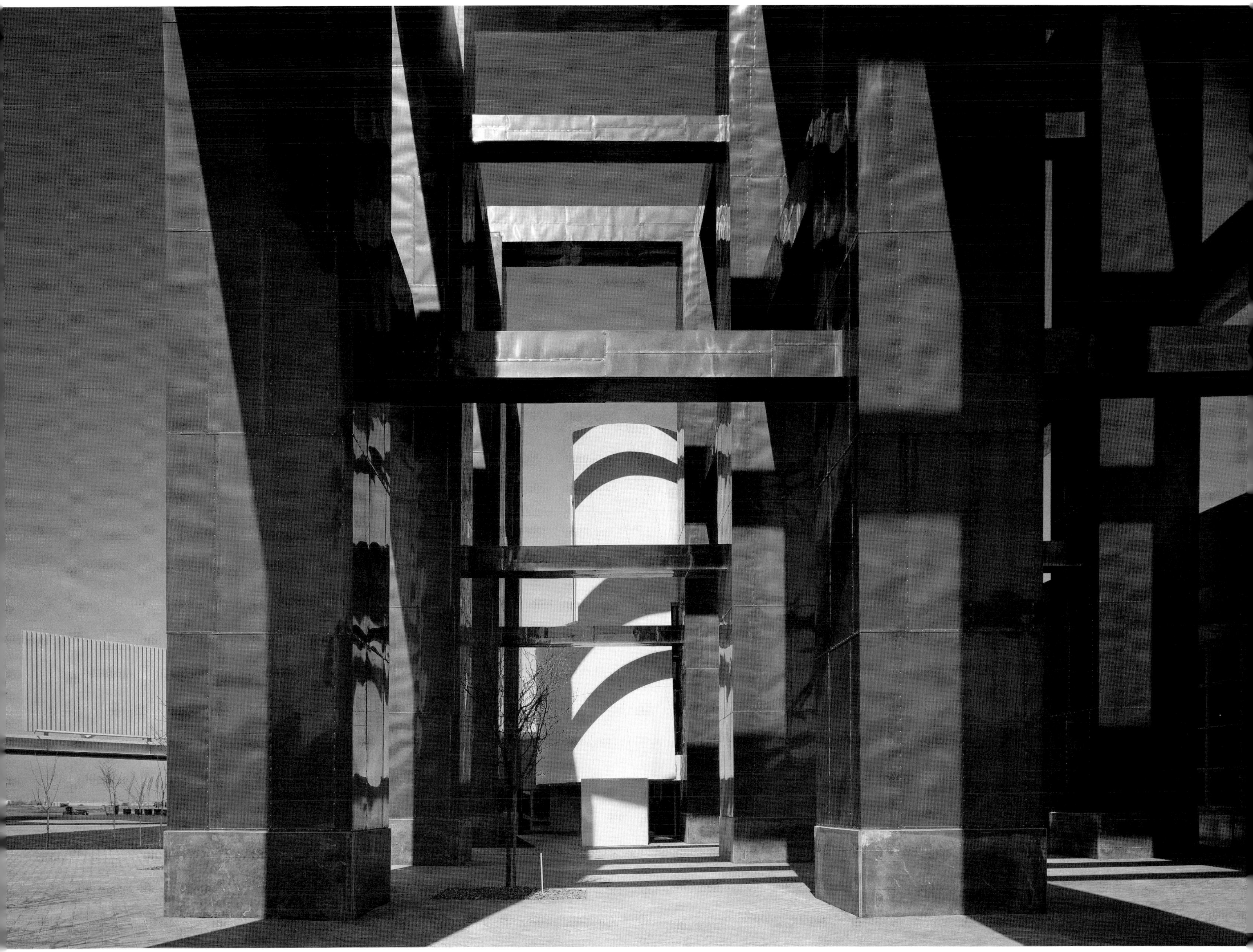

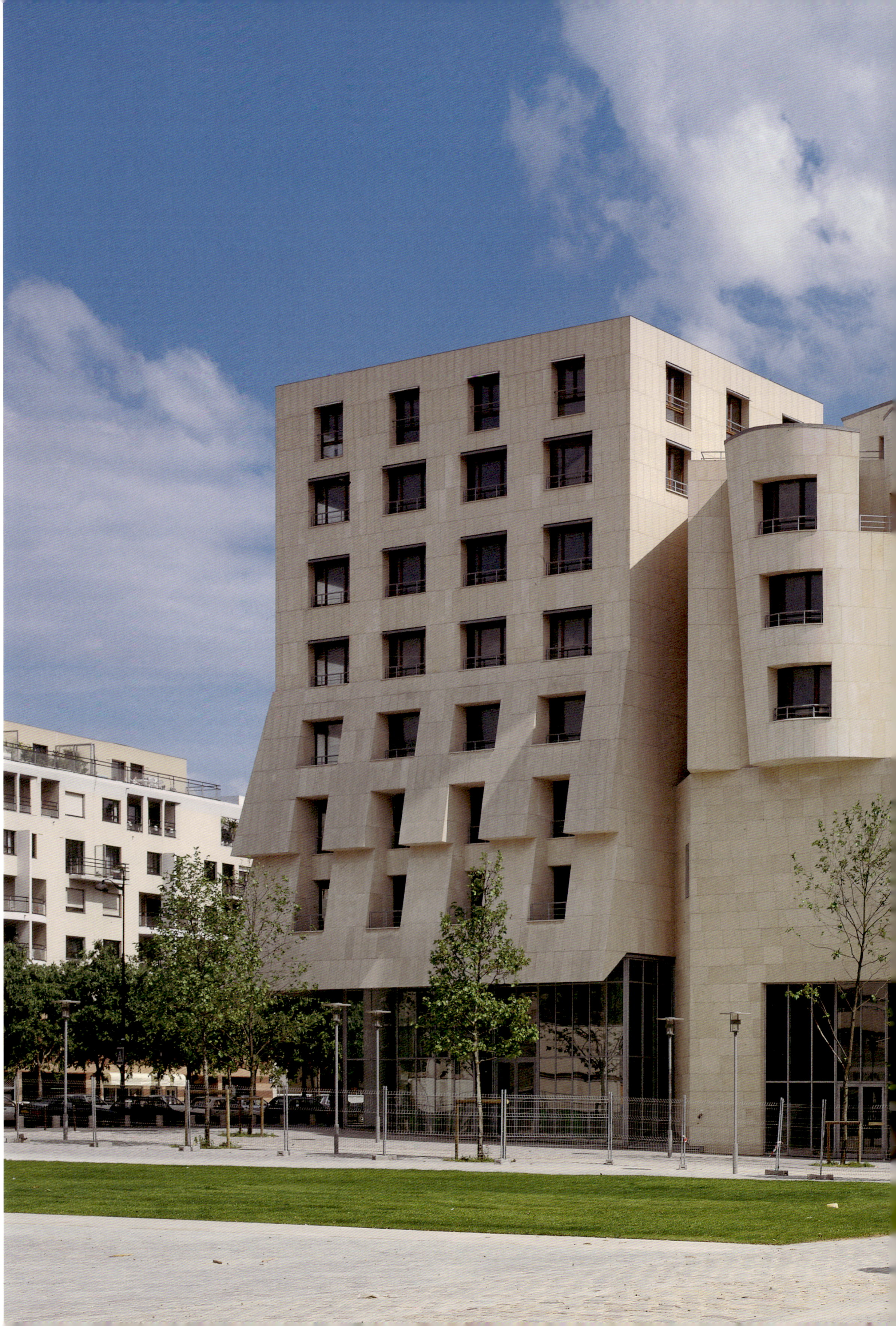

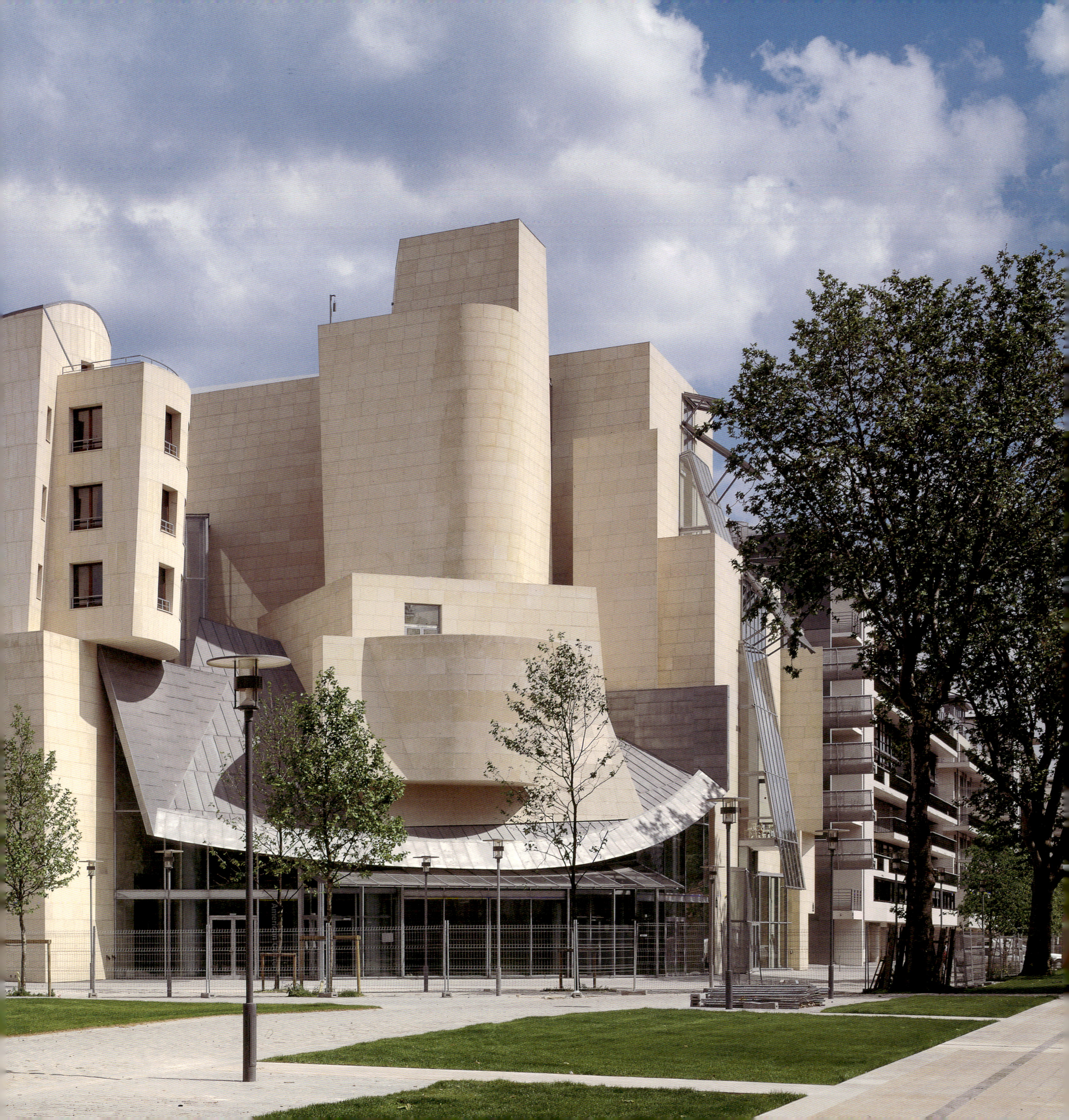

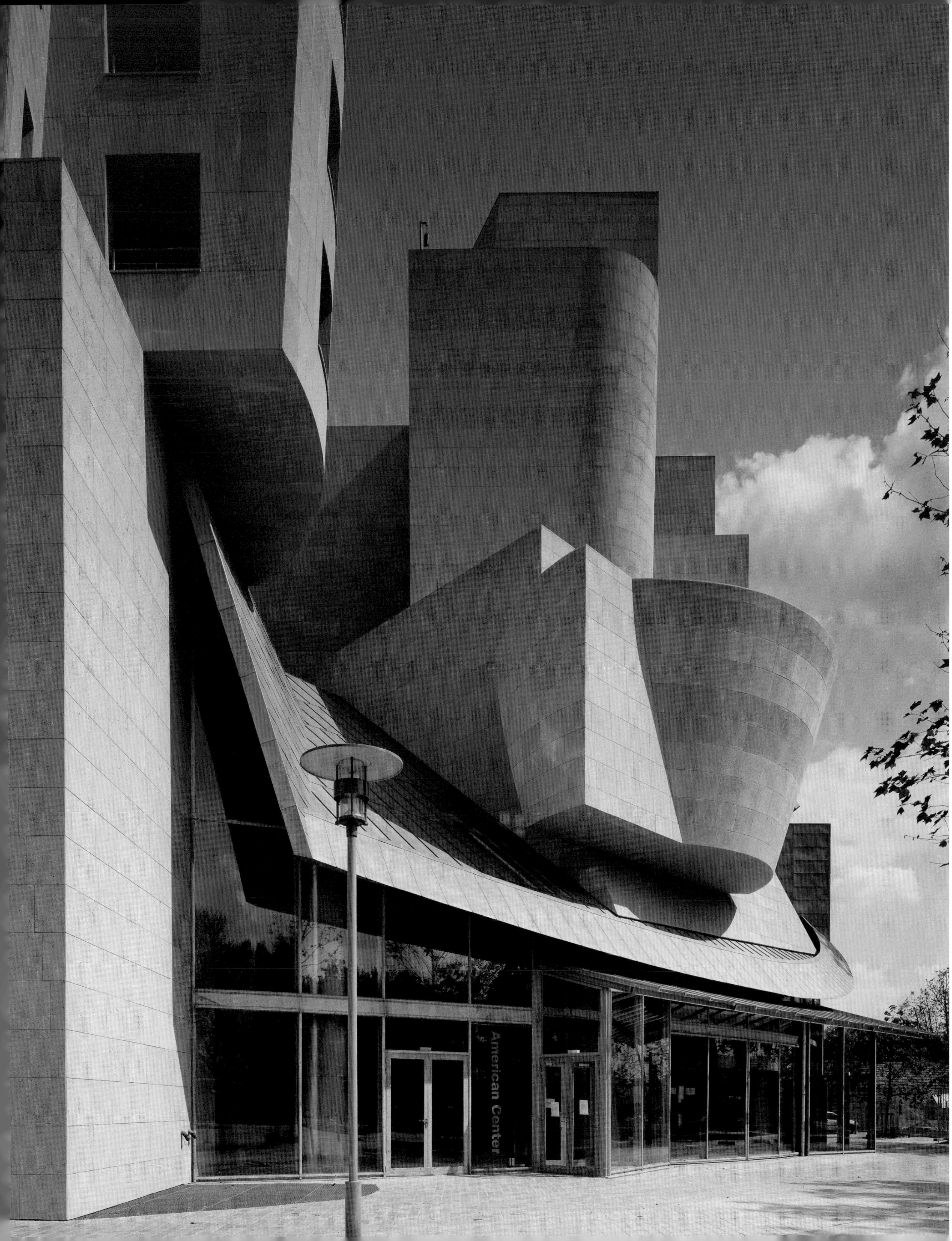
American Center

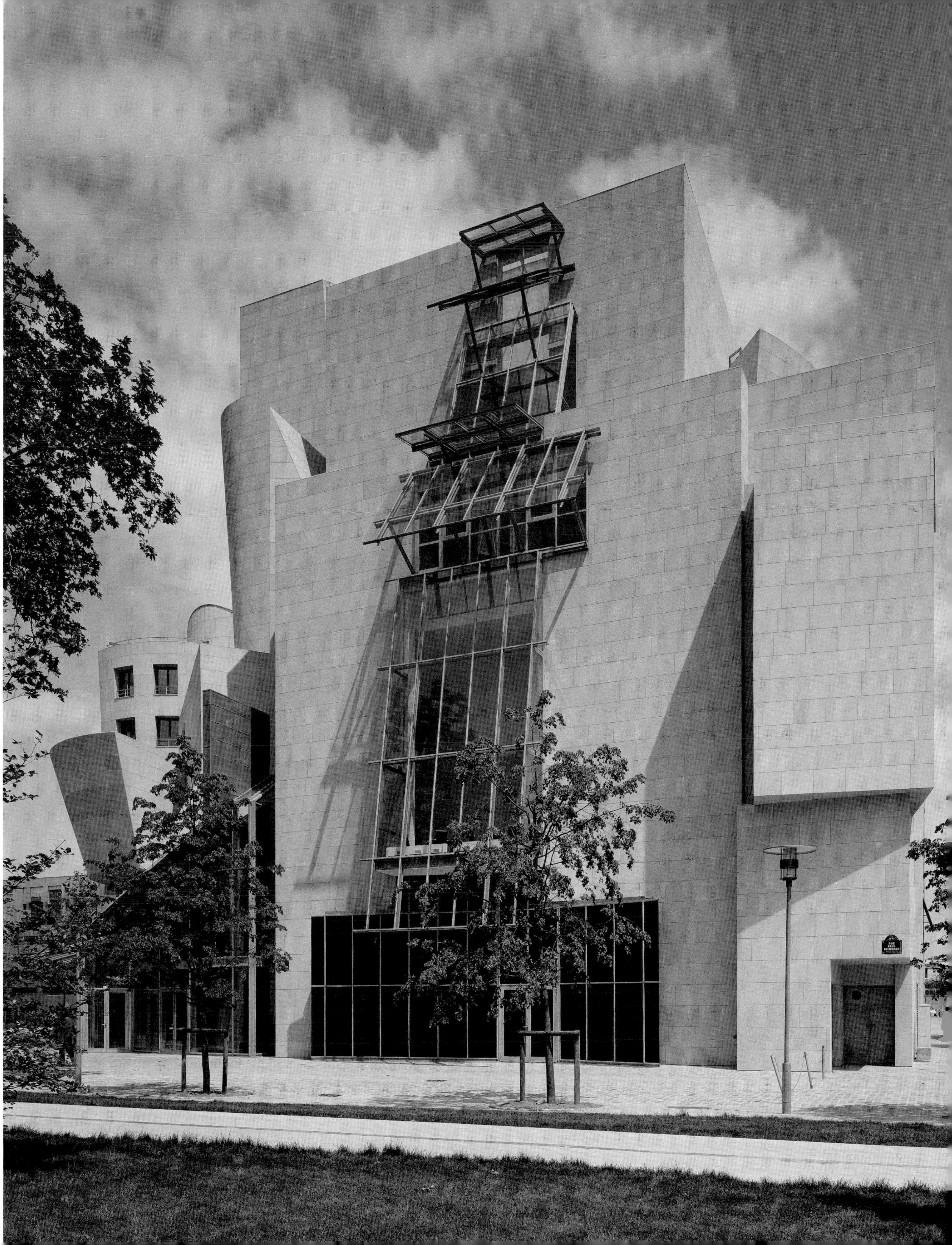

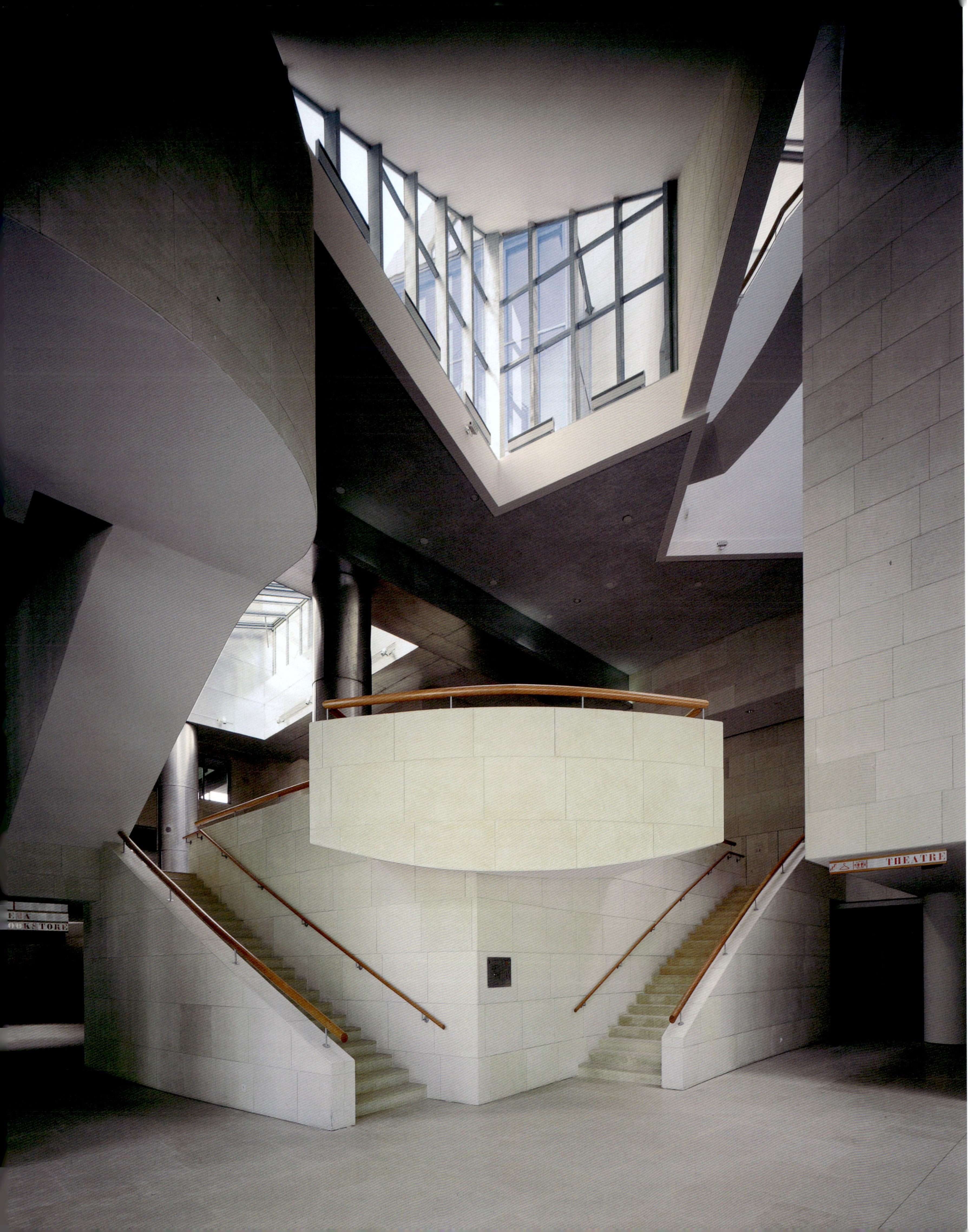
THEATRE

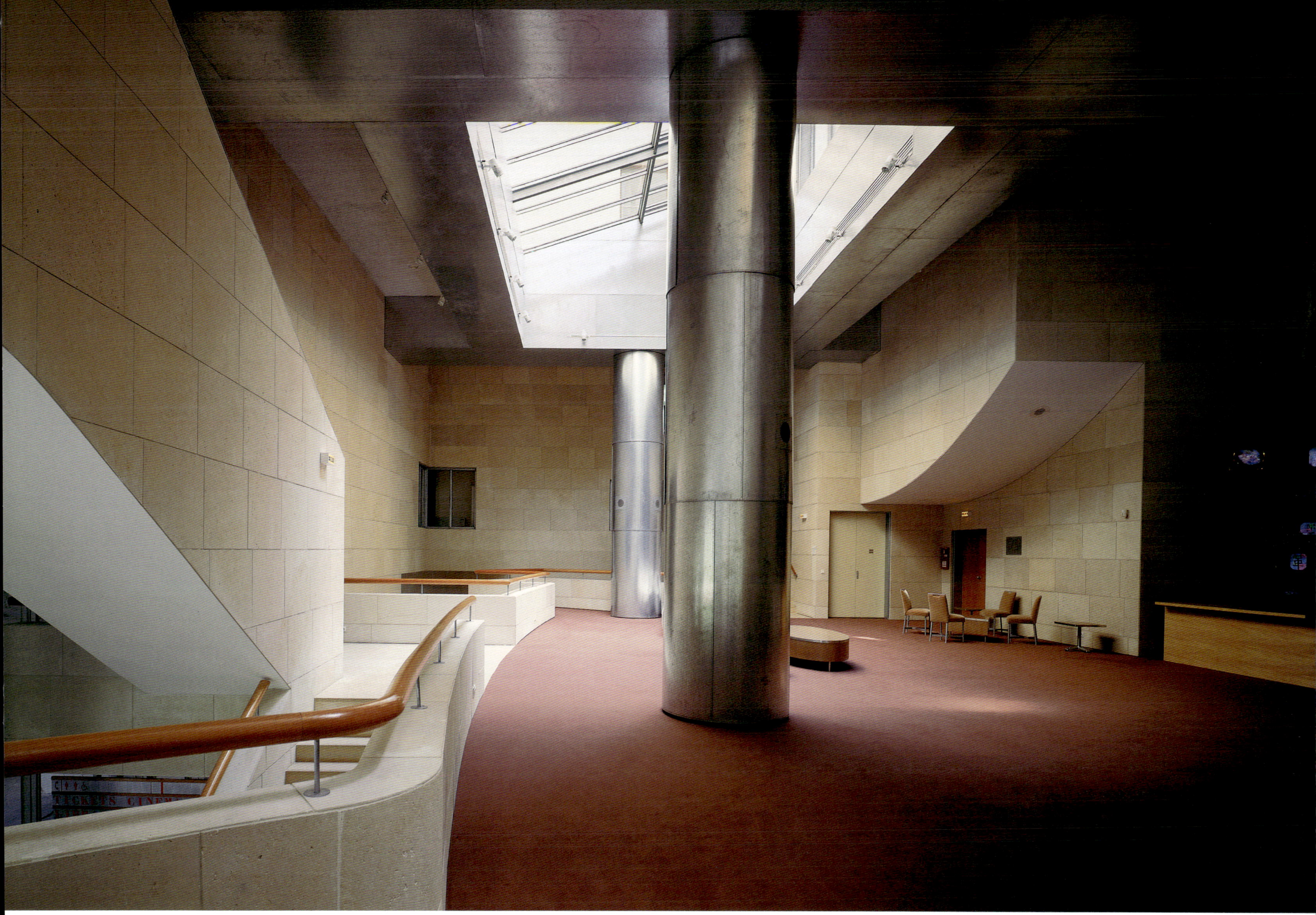

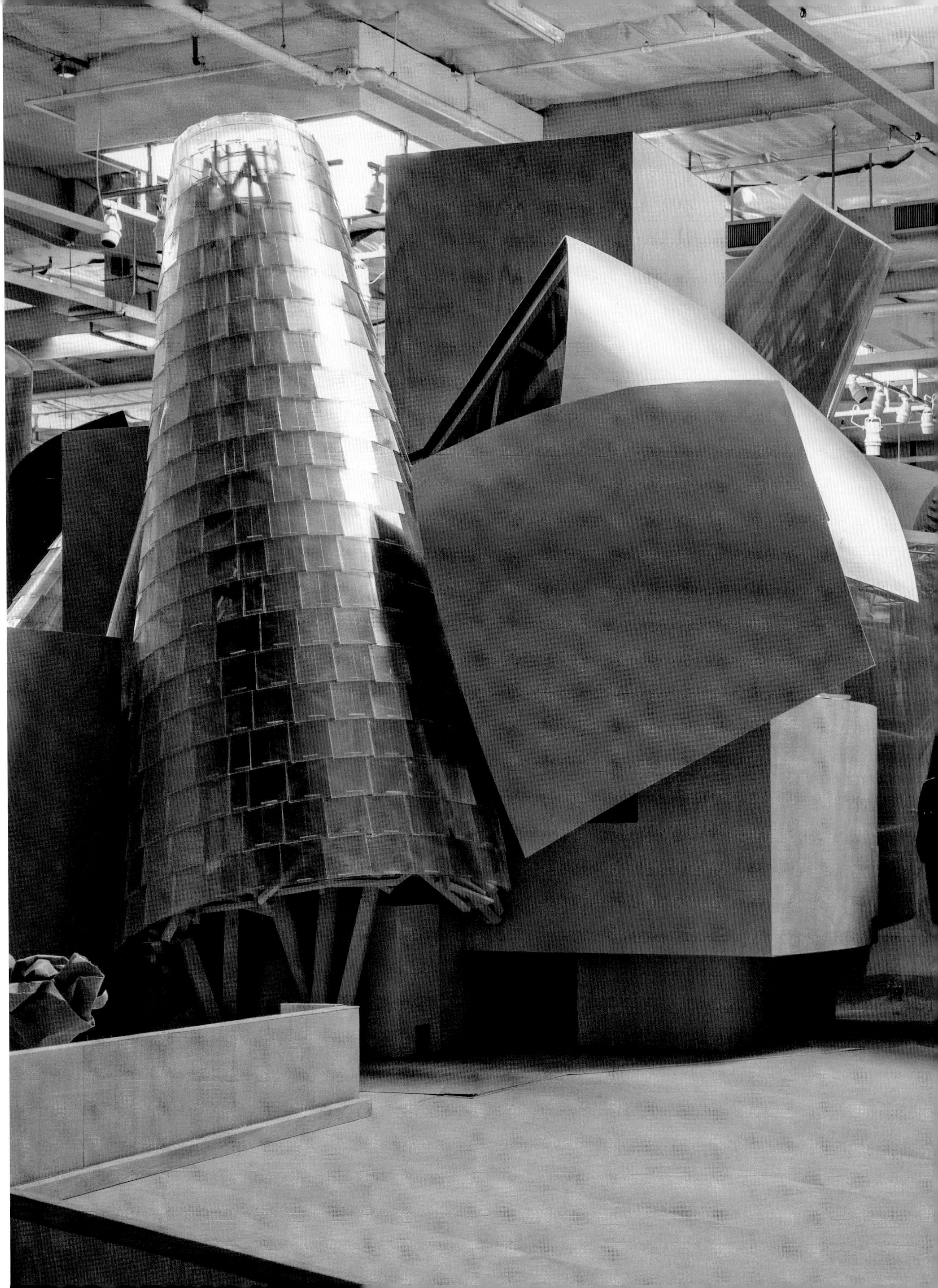

GUGGENHEIM ABU DHABI 2006–

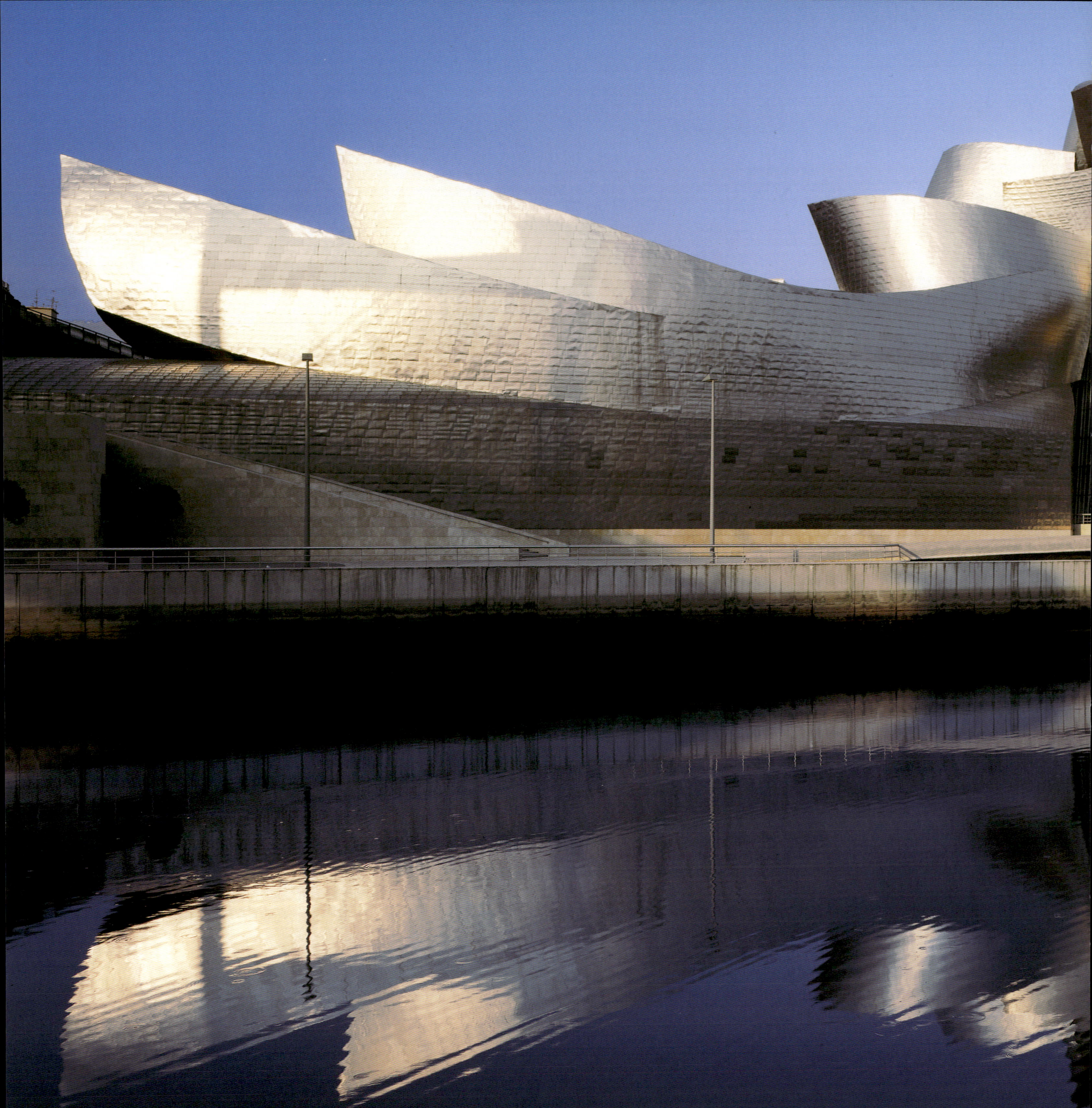

GUGGENHEIM BILBAO MUSEUM 1991-97

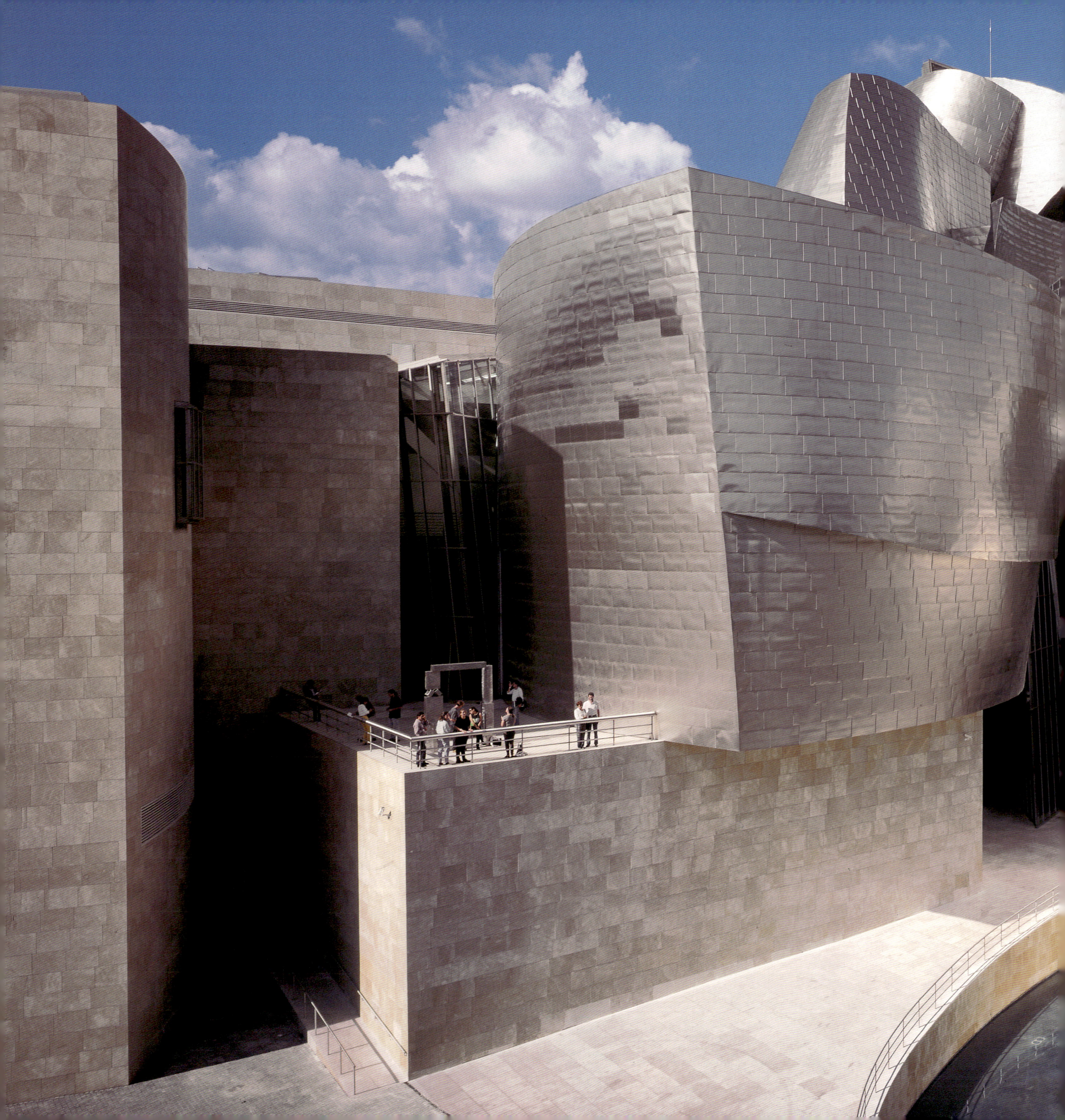

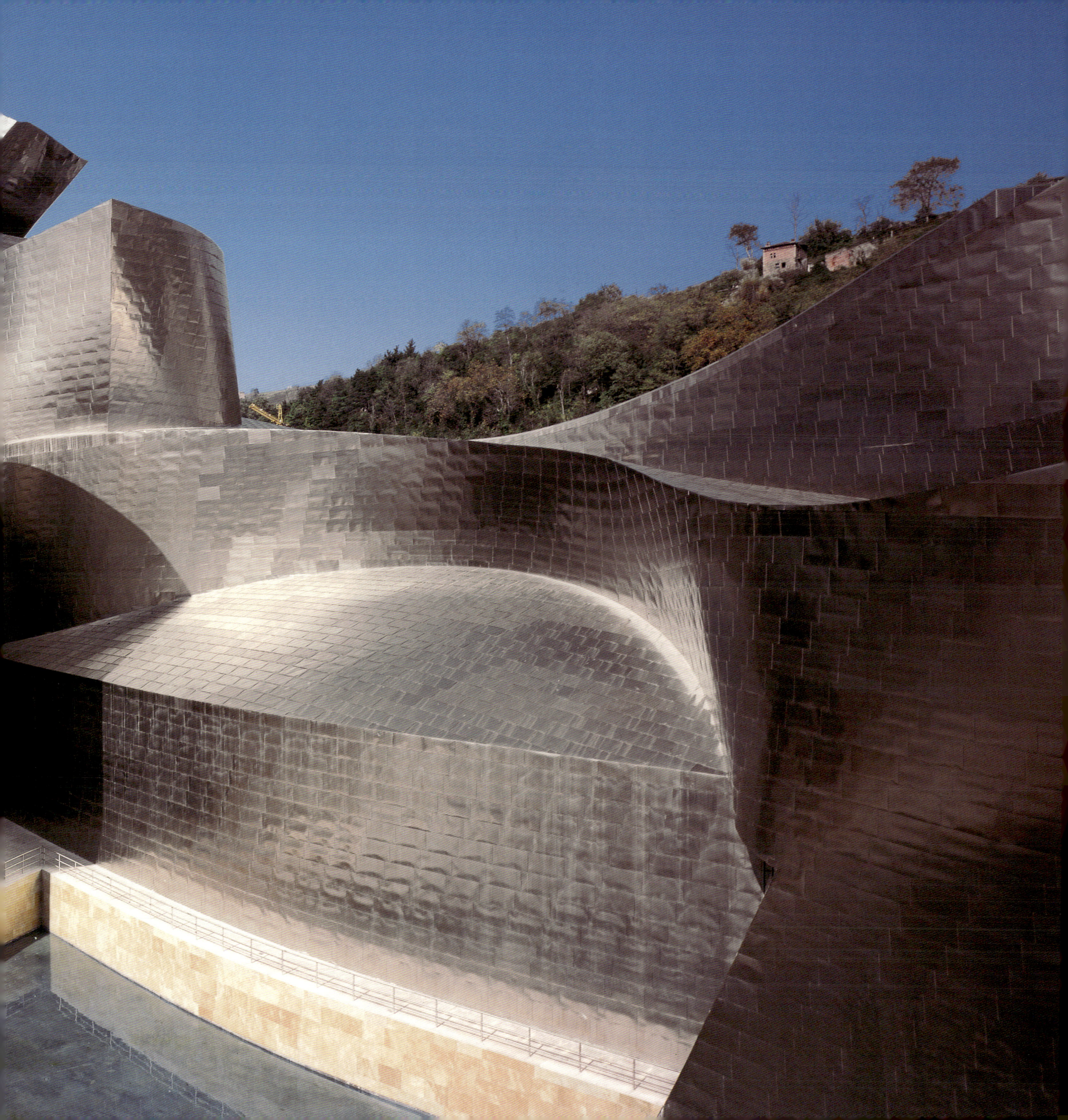

104

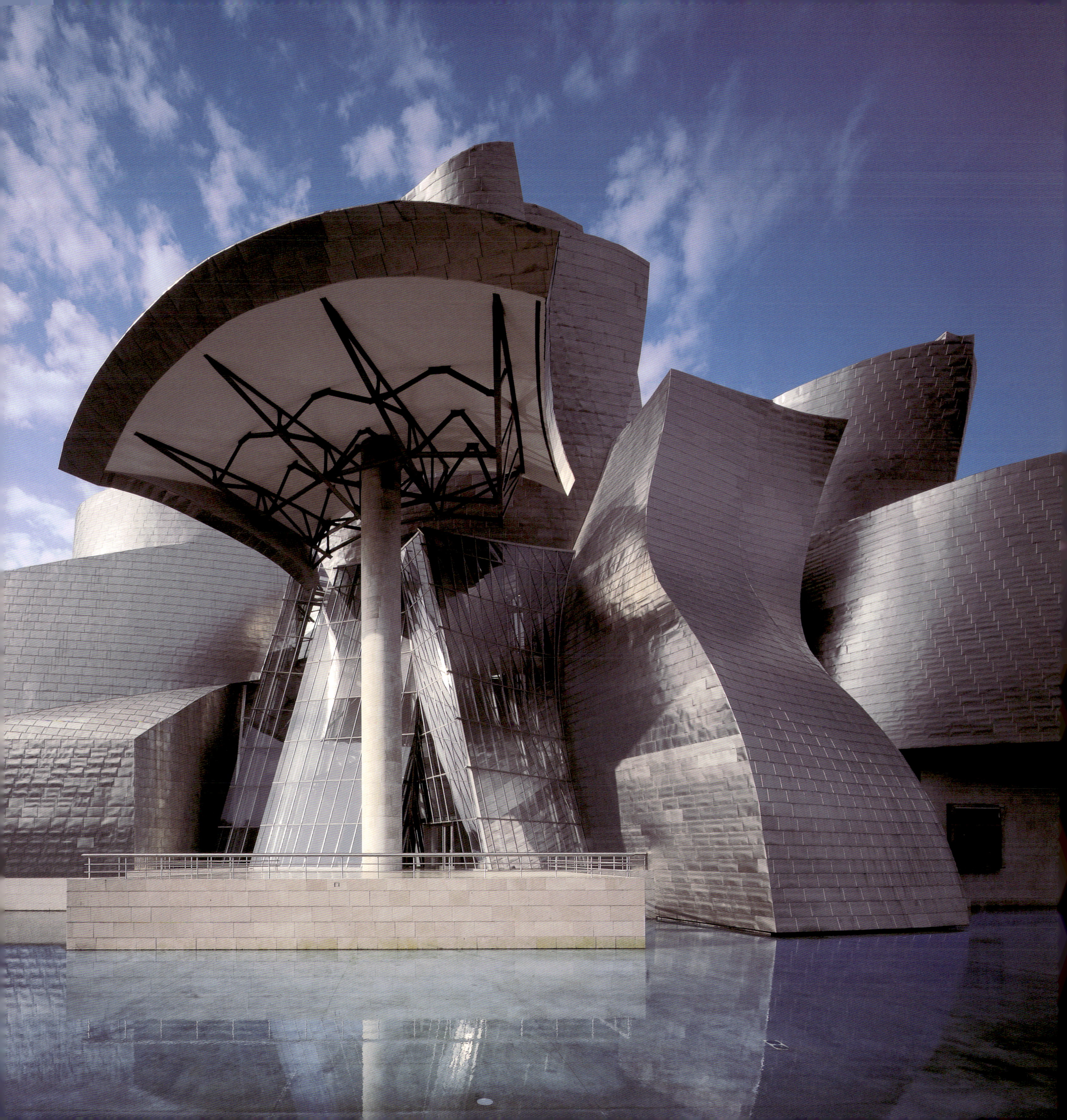

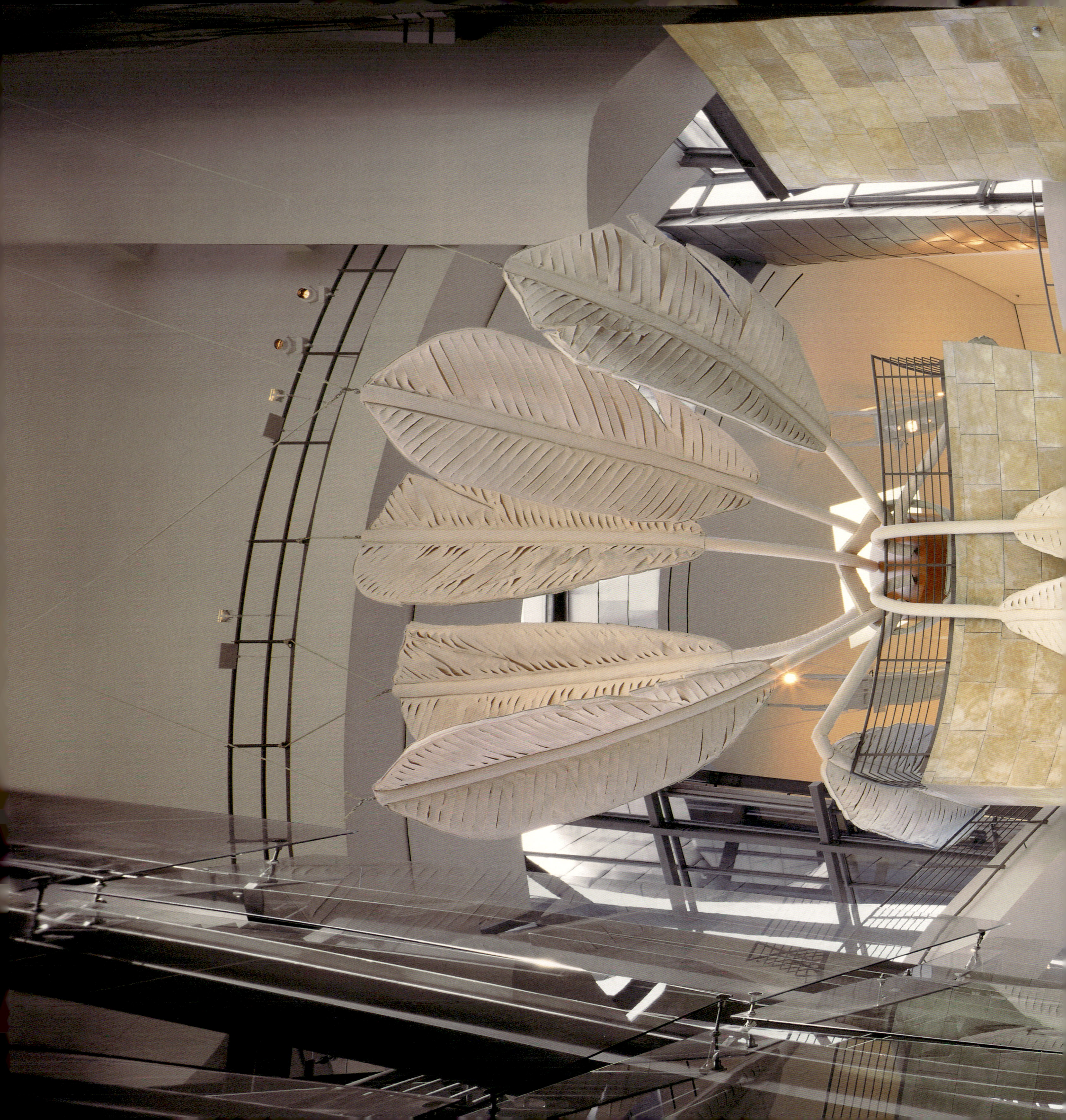

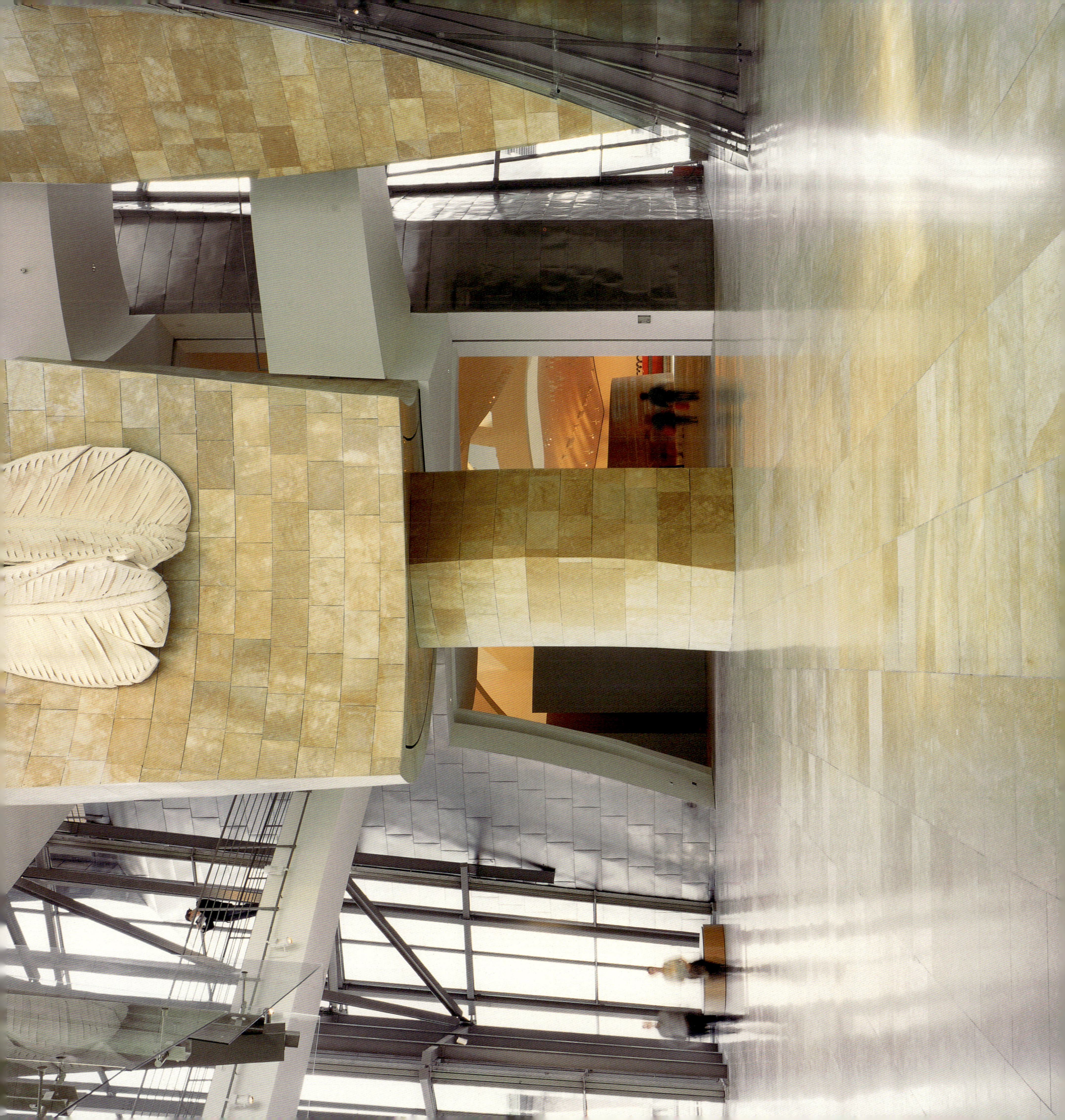

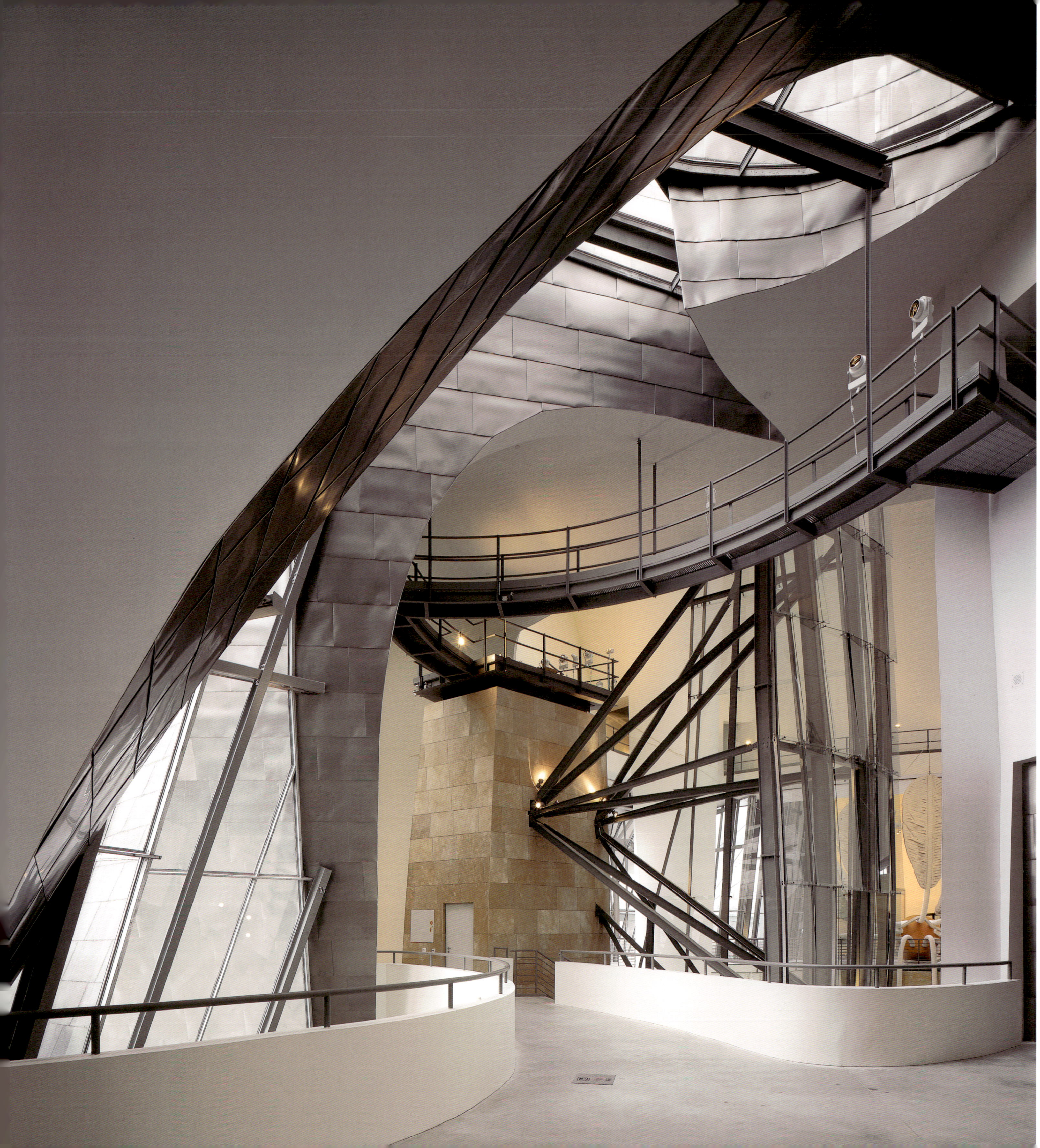

109

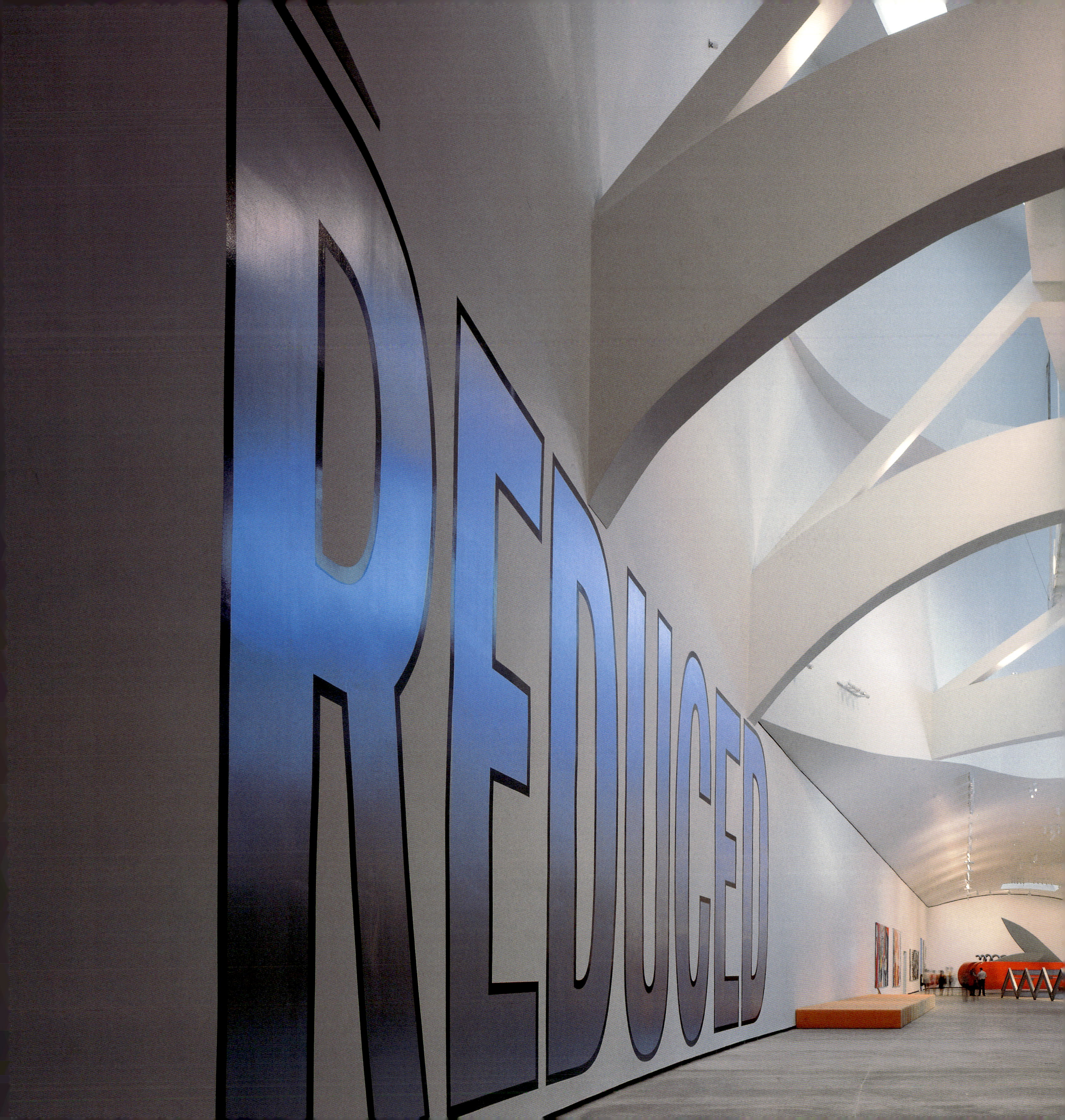
REDUCED

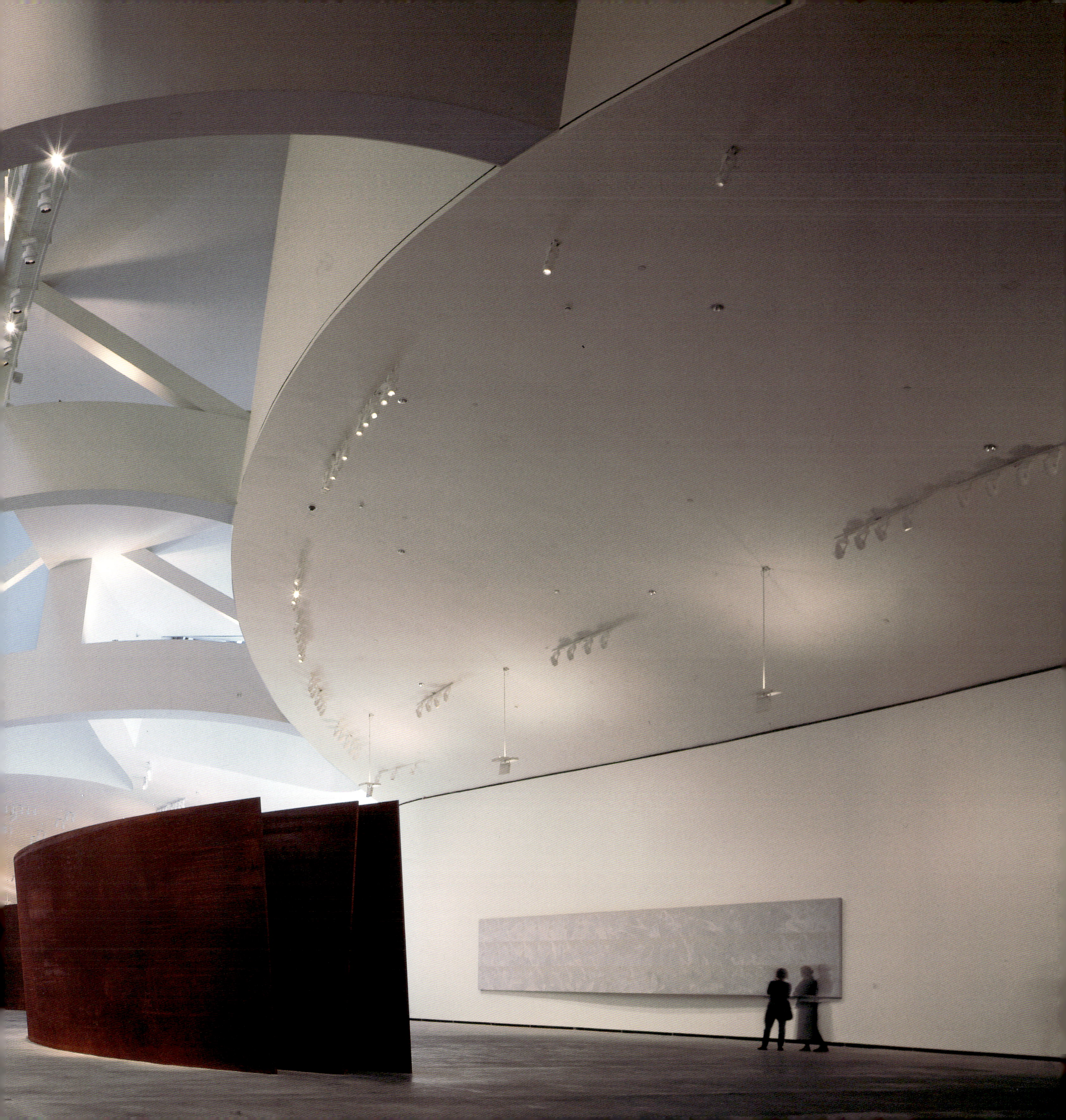

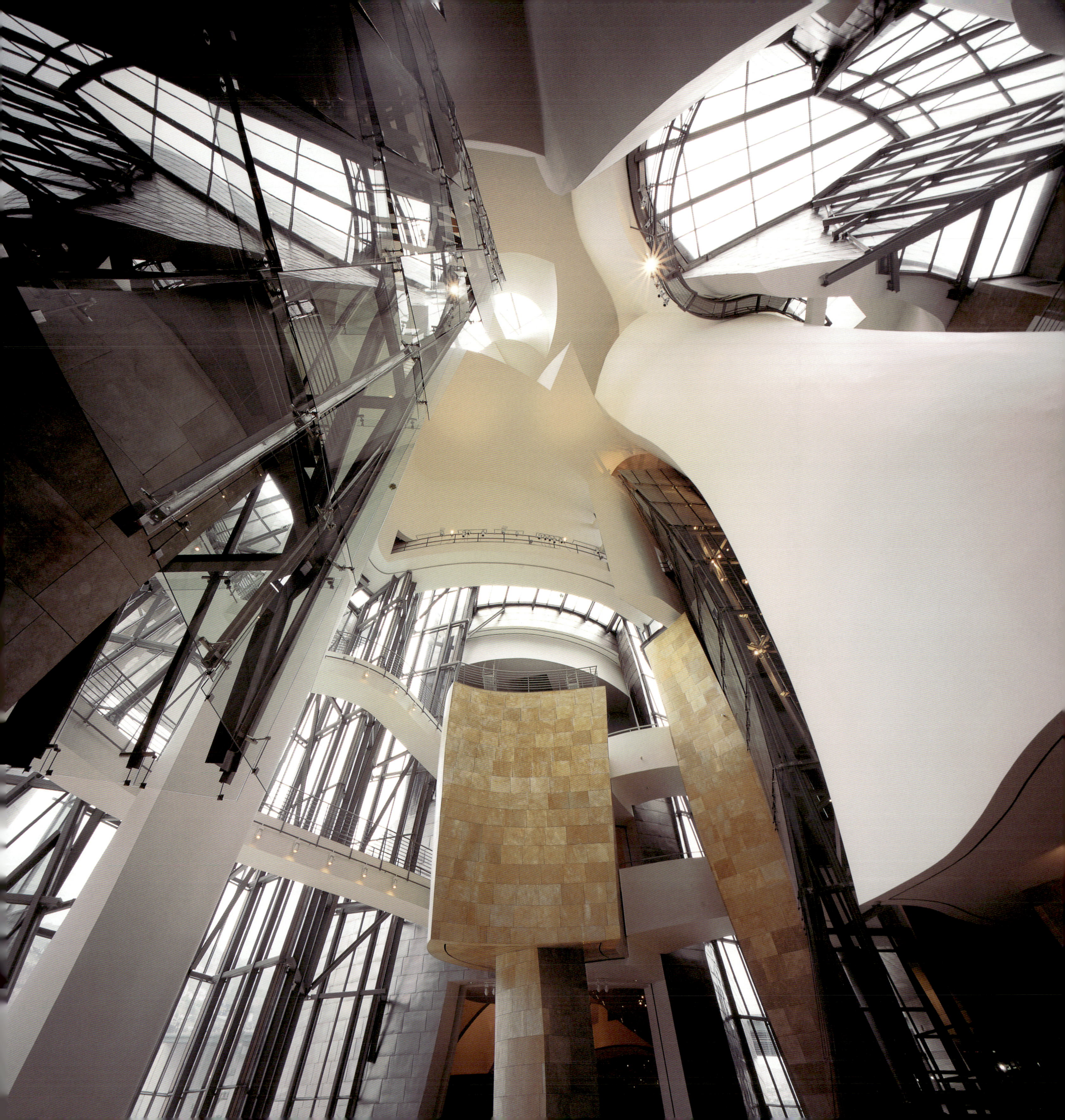

p.7-15

VITRA INTERNATIONAL FURNITURE
DESIGN MUSEUM

1987-89
Weil am Rhein, Germany

p.16-21

UNIVERSITY OF MINNESOTA ART
BUILDING AND TEACHING MUSEUM

1990-93
Minneapolis, Minnesota, U.S.A.

p.22-23

WINTON GUEST HOUSE

1983-87
Wayzata, Minnesota, U.S.A.

p.24-25

NEW WORLD SYMPHONY

2003-11
Miami Beach, Florida, U.S.A.

p.26-29

CHIAT/DAY MAIN STREET

1985-91
Venice, California, U.S.A.

p.30-39

WALT DISNEY CONCERT HALL

1989-2003
Los Angeles, California, U.S.A.

p.40-45

CALIFORNIA AEROSPACE MUSEUM
AND THEATER

1982-84
Los Angeles, California, U.S.A.

p.46-53

GEHRY RESIDENCE

1977-78, 1991-94
Santa Monica, California, U.S.A.

p.54-55

UNIVERSITY OF TOLEDO
ART BUILDING

1990-92
Toledo, Ohio, U.S.A.

p.56-61

HOTEL AT MARQUES DE RISCAL

1998-2006
El Ciego, Spain

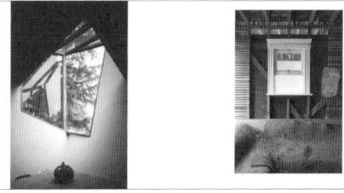

p.62-63

VILA OLIMPICA

1989-92
Barcelona, Spain

p.64-69

RAY AND MARIA STATA CENTER FOR COMPUTER, INFORMATION AND INTELLIGENCE SCIENCES, MASSACHUSETTS INSTITUTE OF TECHNOLOGY

1998-2004
Cambridge, Massachusetts, U.S.A.

p.70-75

EXPERIENCE MUSIC PROJECT

1995-2000
Seattle, Washington, U.S.A.

p.76-77

LOYOLA LAW SCHOOL,
LOYOLA MARYMOUNT UNIVERSITY

1978-91
Los Angeles, California, U.S.A.

p.78-79

IOWA ADVANCED TECHNOLOGY LABORATORIES BUILDING

1987-92
Iowa City, Iowa, U.S.A.

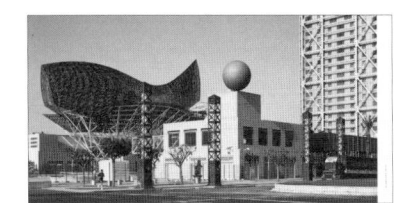

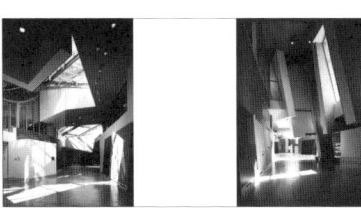

p.80-87

NOVARTIS CAMPUS GEHRY BUILDING

2003-09
Basel, Switzerland

p.88-91

HERMAN MILLER, INC., WESTERN REGION MANUFACTURING & DISTRIBUTION FACILITY

1987-89
Rocklin, California, U.S.A.

p.92-97

AMERICAN CENTER

1988-94
Paris, France

p.98-99

GUGGENHEIM ABU DHABI

2006-
Abu Dhabi, United Arab Emirates

p.100-112

GUGGENHEIM BILBAO MUSEUM

1991-97
Bilbao, Spain

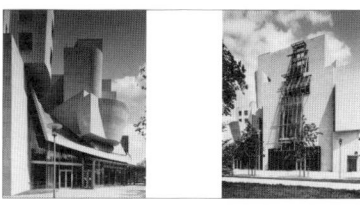

Frank O. Gehry

Born in Toronto, Canada in 1929. Raised in Toronto and moved with his family to Los Angeles in 1947. Received Bachelor of Architecture degree from the University of Southern California in 1954, and studied City Planning at the Harvard University Graduate School of Design.

    Established private practice in Los Angeles in 1962, after working with architects, Victor Gruen and Pereira & Luckman in Los Angeles and with André Remondet in Paris, France. Now, President of Gehry Partners, LLP, Los Angeles, U.S.A.

    Received the Pritzker Architecture Prize in 1989, the Praemium Imperiale Award in 1992, the National Medal of Arts, the Friedrich Kiesler Prize in 1998, the American Institute of Architects Gold Medal in 1999, and the Royal Institute of British Architects Gold Medal in 2000, the Golden Lion Lifetime Achievement Award at the Venice Biennale in 2008 and le Commandeur de l'Ordre National de la Legion d'Honneur in 2014.

Yukio Futagawa

Born in Osaka, Japan in 1932. Graduated from architecture course at the Miyakojima Technical Senior High School, majored in History of Art at Faculty of Letters, Arts and Sciences, the Waseda University and graduated in 1956. Published 10-volume of "Minka—Traditional Japanese Houses" which won the Cultural Award from the Mainich Publishing Company in 1959.

    In 1970, established the architectural publisher, A.D.A. EDITA Tokyo Co., Ltd.. From it now on, it continues to publish a large variety of architectural publications, such as GA DOCUMENT, GA HOUSES and GA JAPAN, especially focusing on modern architecture from all around the world including "GA (Global Architecture)" series (77-volume), "the monograph of the works of Frank Lloyd Wright" (12-volume). Died in 2013.

    Won numerous honors for his work, the AIA in 1975, the Japanese Ministry of Education in 1984, the International Union of Architects (UIA) in 1985 and all. Received Japanese Government, a Purple Ribbon Medal in 1997, the Order of the Sacred Treasure, Gold Rays with Rosette in 2005.

フランク・O・ゲーリー

1929年カナダ，トロント生まれ。1947年，家族と共にロサンゼルスへ移り住むまでトロントで過ごす。1954年，南カリフォルニア大学建築学科で学位を得た後，ハーバード大学デザイン大学院で都市計画を学ぶ。

    その後，ロサンゼルスのヴィクター・グルーエン，ペレイラ&ラックマンや，フランス・パリのアンドレ・ルモンデの事務所を経て，1962年に独立。ロサンゼルスに事務所を構える。現在，ゲーリー・パートナーズ所長。

    1989年プリツカー賞，1992年高松宮殿下記念世界文化賞，1998年アメリカ国民芸術勲章，フレデリック・キースラー賞，1999年アメリカ建築家協会ゴールドメダル，2000年英国王立建築家協会ゴールドメダル，2008年ヴェネツィア・ビエンナーレ生涯業績部門金獅子賞，2014年レジオンドヌール勲章コマンドゥールなど，数々の世界的な賞を受賞。

二川幸夫

1932年大阪市生まれ。大阪市立都島工業高校建築科卒業。早稲田大学文学部で美術史を専攻，1956年卒業。『日本の民家』全10巻を刊行し，1959年，同書にて毎日出版文化賞受賞。

    1970年，建築書籍の編集，出版を専門とする，A.D.A. EDITA Tokyo Co., Ltd.を設立。『GA』シリーズ(既刊77巻)，『フランク・ロイド・ライト全集』(全12巻)をはじめ，定期刊行物『GA DOCUMENT』『GA HOUSES』『GA JAPAN』など，世界の現代建築を中心に出版。2013年没。

    1975年アメリカ建築家協会(AIA)賞，1984年芸術選奨文部大臣賞，1985年国際建築家連合(UIA)賞など受賞多数。1997年紫綬褒章，2005年旭日小綬章受賞。

GEHRY×FUTAGAWA 〈普及版〉

2015年9月25日発行

写真：二川幸夫
編集：二川由夫
デザイン：関拓弥

印刷・製本：大日本印刷株式会社
制作：GA design center
発行：エーディーエー・エディタ・トーキョー
151-0051 東京都渋谷区千駄ヶ谷3-12-14
TEL.(03)3403-1581(代)

禁無断転載

ISBN978-4-87140-494-5 C1052